THE NEW ENGLAND RESEARCH SERIES: 2
*Sponsored by The New England Council, and
Published by Wesleyan University Press*

The Dynamics of Growth in New England's Economy, 1870–1964

The Dynamics of Growth

in New England's Economy,

1870-1964

BY

ROBERT W. EISENMENGER

Wesleyan University Press

MIDDLETOWN, CONNECTICUT

Library of Congress Catalog Card Number: 66–23926
Manufactured in the United States of America
First edition

To my daughters Anne, Katherine, and Lisa

CONTENTS

Figures

TABLES

ACKNOWLEDGMENTS

This book is an adaptation of a Ph.D. thesis that I submitted to the Economics Department of Harvard University in 1963. The thesis in its original form and this revised version have greatly benefited from the help I have received from numerous people. I am particularly indebted to:

Dr. George H. Ellis, President of the Federal Reserve Bank of Boston, who has given me the necessary time to work on this book.

Mrs. Joan T. Poskanzer, formerly of the Bank's research staff, for collecting and organizing much of the basic data and for providing editorial advice on all aspects of this book.

Mrs. Ruth B. Norr, Mrs. Mabelle B. Tucker, Miss Marylu Hayden, and other members of the Bank's research staff for helping in various ways.

Professor James S. Duesenberry, my adviser at Harvard University, who helped review and edit, and who provided ideas for my original thesis as well as this book.

Professor John T. Dunlop, who provided very helpful criticism on several chapters.

My wife for her patience, endurance, and editorial assistance.

The Dynamics of Growth in New England's Economy,
1870–1964

Chapter I

INTRODUCTION

The Problem

THE history of New England shows that economic growth can be sustained in a poorly endowed region which is an integral part of a very well endowed national economy.

New England has few natural resources or locational features to attract and support industry and agriculture. Except for pulpwood, limestone, and granite, the region contains no substantial sources of raw materials, and most of the area's agricultural land is useful primarily because of its nearness to population centers and not because of its inherent productivity. Manufacturing firms must pay, on the average, about 35 per cent more for industrial fuel and about 15 per cent more for electrical energy than firms in the rest of the country. Construction costs are also higher here than in most other regions. Finally, manufacturers have a cost disadvantage when shipping to the rapidly growing consumer markets in the Midwest and Far West.

In the eighteenth and nineteenth centuries New England's ports played a leading role in world trade and provided substantial support for the region's economy. This is no longer true. The ports of New York, Baltimore, and Philadelphia are very large, have excellent rail connections, and offer shippers faster service and a more diversified range of auxiliary services. As a result, they now handle the lion's share of the general merchandise import-export business on the Atlantic seaboard.

The presence of numerous seaports permits New England firms to import raw materials and semifinished products from abroad. Sugar, gypsum, wool, wood pulp, leather, hides, steel-mill products, and chemicals are imported in moderate quantities, partially offsetting the dearth of raw materials within the region. However, a national fuels

3

policy drastically restricts imports of petroleum products (other than residual oil), largely eliminating one of the region's most significant locational advantages. New Englanders, as of 1965, were paying some 200 million dollars more for petroleum products each year than they would if they had free access to world oil markets.

Chapter II provides much additional information about New England's problems. For example, it shows that living costs and taxes are significantly higher there than in most other areas. In addition, the region's rugged climate is generally not attractive to the growing numbers of retired people. Manufacturers and other businessmen cannot hope for the appearance of a large consumer market such as that which developed during the last fifteen years in Florida and the Southwest.

Altogether, it might appear that New England has few locational advantages and that it no longer has any reason for being an important economic and population center. Why, then, does it continue to grow? Why has per capita income in the region averaged 10 per cent higher than that in the nation in recent years? If New England suffers from so many locational disadvantages, it would seem logical for industry and population to move to a place that is better endowed. The region would then have a population decline. The fact is, however, that the population of New England and each of its constituent states has increased almost continuously for the last hundred years, despite the emigration of farmers in the nineteenth century and the loss of much of the textile industry to the South in the twentieth century. Furthermore, in recent years the unemployment rate has been lower in New England than in the United States as a whole.

The Explanation

How can this paradox be explained? Chapters III through VII suggest much of the answer.

Chapter III shows that manufacturers and other employers in New England generally enjoy a wage-rate advantage over similar employers hiring similar labor in other parts of the country. This wage advantage often amounts to 10 per cent or more of wage costs. In some industries this is equivalent to 5 per cent or more of total production costs, an advantage that often makes up for the raw-material and shipping advantages of manufacturing employers in other regions.

Despite low wage rates, New England's level of per capita income has been 10 per cent above the national average in recent years. Chapter III shows that two factors explain much of this paradox.

The region's industrialization and urbanization create a great variety of job opportunities, particularly for women. As a result, the labor-force participation rate is about 2.5 per cent above that in the nation. Since a larger proportion of the population is employed, the earnings of the employed are divided among fewer dependents. For this reason, New England's level of per capita income is higher than it would be if the same proportion of population worked there as work in the nation as a whole.

New Englanders also benefit from substantial property income. Much of this income arises from inherited wealth originally created in the nineteenth century, when the region had a head start on industrialization and trade.

Chapters IV and V analyze postwar manufacturing wage movements in New England labor markets in order to clarify a controversial area of wage theory. For years, economists have disagreed about which factors determine and maintain interarea wage differentials. Some economists believe that these wage differentials exist because of differing supply-and-demand situations in local labor markets; for example, areas of chronic surplus labor have low wage rates. They also believe that differentials would be eliminated if workers would move quickly and easily from areas of labor surplus to those of shortage. Other economists claim that interarea differentials are best explained by industrial composition. They point out that certain industries pay high wages, wherever they are located; others pay low wages in all locations. They conclude that the level and structure of wage rates are largely determined by the composition of industry which happens to be located in each labor market.

Chapter V provides some support for the industrial-composition theory. Most of the evidence, however, favors a variant of the classical supply-demand explanation. In New England there has been a steady movement of population from stagnant low-wage areas to higher-wage areas. There has also been a steady out-migration of young native-born persons and a steady inflow of foreign-born persons from low-wage areas throughout the world. Nevertheless, there has been very little *net* migration from the region as a whole. Furthermore, in most depressed urban areas, the natural population increase has overwhelmed out-migration. The final result has been a steady growth of population and labor force in almost every decade in every state in New England since 1870. Similar growth has taken place in almost all the region's metropolitan areas. Thus, migration statistics suggest that New England's labor force has not responded sufficiently quickly and easily to eliminate interregional and interarea wage differentials.

Chapter V also shows that those labor markets in New England which have had substantial unemployment during the postwar period have had declining wages relative to the national average; those with little unemployment have maintained wages above the national average or have had rising relative wages. Furthermore, the chapter demonstrates that New England's industrial structure shifted into higher-paying industries at a faster rate during the postwar period than did the national structure. Despite this fact, New England's manufacturing wage rates *declined* relative to those in the nation. In other words, the negative impact of unemployment and the lack of sufficient migration (the determinants of wages in the classical theory) overwhelmed the positive impact of a relatively fast shift toward high-wage industries (the determinant of wages in the industrial-composition theory) to bring about a declining relative manufacturing wage level in the region.

A wage-cost advantage is more important in a labor-intensive industry than in a resource-based industry or a capital-intensive industry. It is not surprising to find, therefore, that employers in New England specialize in the type of economic activity that requires a labor-intensive technology. Chapter VI shows that the electronics industry and the other research-and-development-oriented metal-working industries which have grown rapidly in the post–World War II period in New England are labor-intensive industries. They require that a large amount of human effort be exerted on a small volume of raw materials to produce a high-value product.

The rapidly growing nonmanufacturing industries in New England are also labor-intensive. Private colleges and universities, research and development laboratories, insurance and other financial institutions, and hospitals all rely on an extensive variety of skilled personnel for their operation. These service industries are so highly developed in New England that many of them are now capable of selling services to individuals, governments, and companies in foreign countries as well as throughout the United States. In recent years, export income earned by these service industries has become an increasingly important influence on the region's growth.

The term "labor-intensive" often has sweatshop connotations. However, most of these new metalworking industries and the technically oriented service industries are highly prized by communities and industrial developers because their skill requirements and wage rates are relatively high. In these respects, they differ considerably from New England's old labor-intensive manufacturing industries such as apparel, shoes, textiles, jewelry, and lumber.

Chapter VII suggests that part of the explanation of New England's continued growth may lie in the personal preferences of the owners and executives of New England–based firms and to growth momentum resulting from external economies and investments of past generations. Most regional manufacturing firms are managed by New Englanders. The heads of these firms generally do not consider relocating their plants to improve their competitive position. In most cases, they adjust to their locational disadvantages by making changes in their product lines. A larger percentage of the New England population works in urban and urbanized areas than in most other regions. As a result, New England firms benefit from agglomeration and spatial-juxtaposition economies that firms located in more sparsely settled regions do not enjoy.

New England firms have long specialized in the metalworking industries and in providing insurance, banking, engineering, consulting, education, and recreation facilities and services. All these activities have a high income elasticity of demand. The natural growth of the United States economy has benefited this type of economic activity in the region.

In summary, this book describes a regional economy which is successfully competing in national markets, even though it suffers from a great variety of locational handicaps. The region's economy enjoys the advantage of a head start. Both labor and management prefer to remain in the region in which they were brought up. In addition, New England benefits from many man-made advantages and external economies and from its increasing specialization in high-skill, technically oriented, labor-intensive industries.

Chapter II

NEW ENGLAND'S COMPETITIVE POSITION

The Nineteenth Century

BEFORE the Civil War, New England, along with the Middle Atlantic states, dominated the manufacturing and commercial economy of the country. In 1840 the southern New England states surpassed almost all others in per capita income originating in commodity production and commerce. In that year the national average was $65 per capita, but Rhode Island ranked first with $118, Massachusetts third with $107, and Connecticut fourth with $91.[1] In 1850 almost a third of United States manufacturing employment was in New England, and 44 per cent was in the adjoining Middle Atlantic region.[2]

Many conditions brought about industrial development at an early date in the New England states. The Port of Boston provided direct access to world markets and was the second most important seaport in the United States.[3] Creative immigrants in New England designed new machinery and developed new methods for producing textiles, shoes, paper, and other manufactured products. New England was unable to compete effectively in agriculture with the developing western states, so that displaced farm workers, along with the flood of immigrants, created a pool of low-cost labor.[4] The resulting tradition of semirural manufacturing in New England developed a labor force familiar with machine processes.[5] The textile and paper industries were attracted by the high-quality water and water power available from the numerous streams in New England. This was particularly true of paper manufacturers. In 1860 New England accounted for about 50 per cent of the value of output of the paper industry in the United States.[6]

Industrialization also was facilitated by the early development of

8

capital markets in New England. Textile manufacturers benefited from being close to financial intermediaries which provided equity capital obtained from mercantile interests. To some extent shrinking returns from foreign trade encouraged investment, particularly in textiles. More important was the favorable profit record on capital stock. As a result, New England textile growth was financed almost exclusively from funds obtained within the region. The total funds involved were large. In 1860, of the total capital investment of 1.0 billion dollars in all industries in the United States, 7 per cent was invested in textiles in New England.[7]

The introduction of a high tariff during the Civil War cut down imports and greatly accelerated manufacturing in the Northeast. Thus, the New England states had high incomes and a head start on industrialization for what were then very understandable locational reasons. They contained the seaports which carried on trade with Europe. They had a plentiful supply of efficient and low-cost labor. They had the wealthy mercantile interests and the regional financial intermediaries to supply equity capital. They had water power, high-quality process water, and the railroad connections with the developing agricultural West.

Recent History

Since 1850 New England has lost most of its locational advantages. Its seaports have surrendered trade to ports with better rail connections. The fertile agricultural lands of the West have been developed. The nation's extensive iron-ore deposits, petroleum deposits, and timberland have been exploited. Large interior rivers have been harnessed for power generation. All the regional capital markets have been linked together, so that profitable firms in every part of the country can obtain funds for rapid expansion. After 1920 immigration was drastically curtailed and with it New England manufacturers' traditional supply of low-cost unskilled labor.

The total impact of all these changes became readily apparent when employment in New England's textile industry started to decline in the nineteen-twenties.[8] The industry was temporarily revived by defense orders during World War II. The big crash came after the war. New England textile employment dropped from 280,000 in 1947 to 170,000 in 1954 and to 99,000 in 1964. During 1949 the average unemployment rate reached new highs in many Massachusetts cities: 26 per cent in Lawrence, 18 per cent in New Bedford, and 12 per cent in Fall River and Lowell. The Providence-Pawtucket, Rhode Island, area had 13 per cent unemployed during the same year.

As a result of this social and industrial disaster, numerous organizations, research groups, and individuals have examined the New England economy.[9] They discovered that the region has an impressive array of locational problems, which are described in the remaining pages of this chapter.

THE COST OF PETROLEUM PRODUCTS (OTHER THAN RESIDUAL OIL)

New Englanders do have one locational advantage: they pay less than the national average for petroleum products (other than residual oil). The retail prices of gasoline and No. 2 heating oil are lower in Boston than in many other major cities throughout the country. In June of 1964 the retail price of gasoline in Boston was about 84 per cent of the average for a group of major United States cities, that of No. 2 fuel oil just under the average. The cost of transporting crude oil from Texas by boat is significantly less than the cost of transporting oil overland to many inland points.

If federal import restrictions on petroleum products (other than residual oil) did not exist, New Englanders would buy petroleum products at even lower prices. The region has easy access to suppliers in South America and the Near East, and producers in these regions are able to deliver oil to the East Coast at prices well below the long-run production costs of domestic producers. As of June 1965, world crude-oil prices (f.o.b. New York City) were more than $1.00 a barrel below domestic prices. The net result is that New Englanders pay some 200 million dollars more for petroleum products each year than they would if they had permanent free access to world oil markets.[10]

HIGH INDUSTRIAL FUEL COSTS

Industrial fuel costs, however, should be listed among New England's locational disadvantages. As measured by the cost of fuel used in electric power generation plants, industrial fuel costs are higher in New England than in any other region of the United States and about 35 per cent higher than in the country as a whole. It also may well be that these statistics underestimate the region's industrial fuel-cost disadvantage. Most electric utility steam plants are located at tidewater, where prices are lowest. At inland locations, industrial fuel prices run 25 to 33 per cent above those at coastal ports.

Industrial fuel is more expensive in New England than in other regions because New England must import its supplies of coal, gas, and residual oil, while other regions are nearer the source of one or more of these fuels. Bituminous coal must be brought to New England by rail or boat from West Virginia and Pennsylvania. Natural gas must be piped more than a thousand miles from southern states. Most of the residual oil used in New England is imported from abroad, and although many buyers find it to be the least expensive industrial fuel,[11] it is not as inexpensive as coal and gas in other parts of the United States where residual oil is the most expensive fuel. Until very recently,* the federal oil-import restriction program has raised the domestic price of residual oil above world prices, and the program has cost New England buyers as much as 20 million dollars in some recent years.[12]

It might be argued, therefore, that federal residual-oil import restrictions have caused industrial fuel costs to be high in New England. If this were true, New England's high industrial fuel cost would be an "artificial" rather than a "natural" locational disadvantage. Certainly it is true that residual-oil prices in the region have been significantly higher than they would have been without restrictions. However, the Western Hemisphere supply of residual oil is limited. And even if additional large quantities of oil had been imported, they probably would have displaced only a small fraction of the total volume of bituminous coal, which is the principal fuel used by public utilities and industry in most Atlantic seaboard states. The result would have been lower residual-oil prices and slightly lower coal prices, but the price of coal could not have dropped substantially because the coal industry has been operating for some years with surplus capacity and depressed profit levels.

The high cost of industrial fuel prevents some types of manufacturing industries from locating in New England. For example, the glass

---

* Federal restrictions on imports of residual oil for the East Coast were removed on Friday, March 25, 1966, by Secretary of the Interior Stewart L. Udall.

and steel industries generally locate near low-cost sources of fuels. However, a few of New England's important industries use substantial quantities of industrial fuel. Fuel costs comprise as much as 6 per cent of total manufacturing costs in the pulp and paper industry,[13] and in parts of the textile industry, fuel costs make up 2 to 3 per cent of total costs.[14] Of course, the electric utility industry consumes large quantities of fuel, but all its costs are passed on to users of electric power. Thus, all consumers of power—residential and commercial as well as industrial users—are affected by the high price of industrial fuel in New England.

HIGH ELECTRIC POWER COSTS

High electric power costs provide a significant locational disadvantage for New England. The region's industrial electric power rates are typically about 15 per cent higher than the national average[15] and are among the highest in the country for an industrialized area. As in the case of fuel costs, however, this is not a serious disadvantage for most of the important industries located in New England.[16] These industries do not use large quantities of electrical energy. A notable exception is the pulp and paper industry. However, many firms in this industry have inherited ownership or control of prime water-power sites.[17]

A number of authorities have argued that a part of the New England–United States differential could be eliminated if proper public policies were instituted. Seymour Harris[18] has pointed up the advantages of integrated river-basin development. Bright[19] and Hughes[20] have suggested that integrated planning and operation of the generation and transmission systems of the region's thirteen large privately owned utilities could result in significant savings. Shipman[21] has suggested that such savings, in the long run, might eliminate one-fourth to one-half of the New England–United States differential.

Recent technological developments have brought rapid changes. Nuclear-powered plants are being installed which, in many parts of the country, can produce power at a lower cost than the most efficient new conventional coal- and oil-fired steam plants. Furthermore, new high-voltage transmission lines can now transmit power with very low line losses for hundreds of miles. As a result, New England's power costs may drop 25 per cent by the year 1972, when they will be closer to the national average.[22] The future trend of power costs, however, does not help explain past economic growth.

THE HIGH COST OF LIVING

Bureau of Labor Statistics studies made in October 1959 showed how the cost of maintaining a specified standard of living for a particular type of family varied among twenty cities in the United States.[23] Among the twenty cities studied, the cost for a city worker's family in Boston was exceeded only by that in Chicago and Seattle. The relative cost for a retired couple living in Boston was even higher and was exceeded only in Chicago.

No similar indices are available for other cities in New England. It is possible, therefore, that Boston's relatively higher costs of maintaining a particular standard of living are not representative of other cities in the region. Authorities in the Boston Regional Office of the Bureau of Labor Statistics believe, however, that the average cost in urban centers in New England is slightly higher than the national average for cities of similar size.[24]

HIGH TRANSPORTATION COSTS

New England manufacturers face a competitive disadvantage in obtaining raw materials and in shipping to most consumer markets in the United States. In many cases, competing manufacturers are located between the New England producer and both his suppliers and his customers.

In the nineteenth century, commodity railroad rates to New England (for raw materials) and class rates from New England (for manufactured products) were relatively low.[25]* The freight-rate structure was deliberately developed to permit producers of raw materials to enjoy low rates when shipping to New England and to allow New England manufacturers to have low freight costs when shipping to the Midwest.

As the national economy developed, shippers in other regions

---

* Class rates apply to only a part of total railroad freight. A larger part of the total is shipped under commodity rates. Historically, interregional differentials on commodity rates have been much less than interregional class-rate differentials. However, the class rates do apply to many manufactured products.

charged that the rate structure was discriminatory. They argued that there should be a uniform system of rail freight charges throughout the country. Over the years, the Interstate Commerce Commission has supported this point of view.

In 1917 class rates in the eastern United States were increased 15 per cent, while rates in other parts of the country were left unchanged. And between 1943 and 1950 the differences between the rates charged in the eastern United States and in other parts of the country were narrowed substantially. In 1943 the average of first-class rates in the southern area was 39 per cent above that in the eastern area, and in the southwestern area the average was 61 per cent higher. By 1950 these percentages had declined to 8 and 17, respectively. Finally, in 1952 the Interstate Commerce Commission established a uniform system of class rates for rail freight throughout the country.

In 1957 Lindahl published a comprehensive analysis of the freight-cost disadvantage for New England producers in a variety of industries.[26] Among the industries he considered were cotton and woolens, shoes and leather, rubber and rubber goods, paper, and metalworking, including steel, brass, bronze, and copper. The study showed that while New England manufacturers sometimes were able to obtain imported raw materials at a slightly lower cost than other domestic manufacturers, they suffered significant cost disadvantages both in obtaining raw materials from domestic sources and in shipping finished products outside the New England–New York area.

TAXES

United States Bureau of the Census data show that per capita state and local tax collections in 1963 were 8 per cent higher in New England than in the United States as a whole. Per capita state and local tax levels in Connecticut and Massachusetts, the most populous states, were 12 to 15 per cent above the national average. Those in Maine and New Hampshire were 13 or 14 per cent below, with only Vermont and Rhode Island levels close to the national figures.[27] However, these data provide no information as to the distribution of the tax burden among individuals, manufacturing firms, and other business enterprises.

A thorough study of state and local taxation of manufacturing firms was made in 1958 by John Strasma for a Harvard doctoral dissertation.[28] Unfortunately, Strasma was able to collect information for only a limited number of cities and towns in Massachusetts, Rhode Island, Connecticut, Illinois, Ohio, Indiana, Missouri, and Maryland.

The data he did collect were comprehensive and, except for employment taxes, included all state and local taxes imposed on manufacturing firms. Specific allowance was made for the assessment policies prevailing in each community. The variance was found to be much greater among communities within a state than among states. Strasma's data also suggest, however, that taxes on manufacturers are heavier in southern New England than in the rest of the country.

Expenditures per pupil in public schools are also considerably higher in industrialized southern New England than elsewhere in the nation.[29] It may well be that the extra money spent on public schools does more to benefit manufacturers than would a substantial reduction in taxes. The availability of a plentiful supply of trained labor is an important competitive advantage for many New England firms. Strasma's data suggest, however, that New England manufacturing firms are now paying for much of this public education.

SOIL RESOURCES

There is some good land in New England. The land in the Connecticut River Valley in Massachusetts is very productive when well fertilized. This is also true of large acreages of potato-producing land classified as "Caribou loam" in Aroostook County, Maine. In general, however, the poor quality of the soils in New England has discouraged farming.

The late Professor John Black has described New England as "a region not even moderately well endowed with natural soil resources."[30] He based this statement on numerous federal and state soil surveys, showing that most of the soils in New England are of poor quality. Almost none of the New England soils is as good as the better soils in the corn belt, and about 35 per cent of the land in New England is so stony that it cannot be profitably farmed.

The net result is that today New England is the most heavily forested region in the United States. Almost 80 per cent of its land has a forest cover.[31] Only 8 per cent of the region's land is in crops, and most of this is farmed only because it is close to markets. In the United States, on the other hand, 33 per cent of the land is forested and 20 per cent is cropland. These facts go a long way in explaining why New England imports most of its food products from other regions.

RAW MATERIALS

Except for pulpwood and common minerals such as granite, basalt, limestone, marble, and slate, New England has a dearth of raw materials. The region does not produce significant quantities of iron, copper, bauxite, gold, silver, or sulphur. All told, the value of mineral production in the six New England states in 1963 amounted to only one-half of 1 per cent of the total national production.[32]

Although almost 80 per cent of the region has a forest cover, New England's forest-products industries are not favorably situated with respect to raw materials. More than half of the private forest-land holdings in New England are in what the U.S. Forest Service classes as "other private ownerships." These owners are not farmers or manufacturers of lumber, pulp and paper, or other wood products but are clubs, business and professional people, housewives, laborers, and other private individuals. In New England, 9½ million of the 15 million acres of land held by these "other private owners" are in holdings of less than 500 acres.[33]

Work done at the Harvard Forest[34] and elsewhere has shown that most of these owners view their forest holdings as a retreat or obtain satisfaction simply from visiting their land occasionally on weekends. In many cases, this type of owner is hostile to forest management because he believes the aesthetic value of his forest will be destroyed if he permits any type of cutting. For these reasons, the available supply of pulpwood and saw timber is considerably less than that shown in the aggregate forest-inventory figures of the U.S. Forest Service.

In addition, the rough New England terrain, the harsh climate, and the high cost of woods labor raise the cost of cutting and moving pulpwood and saw logs into the mills. As a result, the delivered cost of pulpwood and saw timber is significantly higher in New England than in the South. United States Bureau of the Census data for the year 1954 show that the cost of hardwood pulpwood delivered at mills was higher in New England than in any other region of the country and about 30 per cent above the national average.[35]

Several industry officials have told the writer that technical advances in logging have enabled New England's pulp and paper industry to improve its competitive position in recent years. It is likely, therefore, that the 1954 census data exaggerate the present cost disadvantage of the region's users of hardwood pulpwood. Unfortunately, more recent cost data are not available.

The census data are also deficient in that no regional cost information is available for spruce and fir, the most valuable pulpwood species in New England. The growing pulp and paper industry in northern New England depends heavily on these species, which are unavailable in most other parts of the country. Spruce-fir wood pulp is valuable because of its unique color characteristics and its great strength. In recent decades, however, improved pulping processes have enabled manufacturers of a wide range of paper products to substitute lower-cost hardwood and southern-pine wood pulp for wood pulp made from spruce and fir.

CONSTRUCTION COSTS

The extra cost involved in bringing building materials into New England pushes up construction costs. A comparison of the total cost (including labor cost) of constructing various types of buildings in twenty large cities throughout the United States indicates that construction costs in Boston run 3 to 5 per cent above the national average.[36] United States Department of Defense data for 1962 showed that construction costs in each New England state were higher than those in most other states.[37] Maine was listed as the highest-cost state in the continental United States. However, all such cost indices suffer from one deficiency: no allowance is made for the more expensive buildings required in an area which has a harsh winter climate. This is a particularly important factor in residential building. It is likely, therefore, that the data comparing twenty large U.S. cities underestimate relative construction costs in Boston.

THE CLIMATE

The only area in New England which has a mild climate is Cape Cod, but the winter weather there is damp and uncomfortable. It is difficult to imagine a large in-migration of retired persons into New England similar to that which has occurred in Florida, Arizona, and New Mexico in the post–World War II period.[38]

Furthermore, some manufacturing firms deliberately avoid areas with harsh winter climates. Cunningham[39] has demonstrated that manufacturers of aircraft (airframes) deliberately select locations which have a mild climate with clear days for flying.

On the other hand, New England's cool summer weather along the shore and its attractive scenery provide the basis for a tourist industry. Similarly, the heavy winter snowfall in interior New England helps enterprises catering to skiers.

On balance, however, New England's rugged climate probably deters economic growth.[40]

FISHING: NO LONGER AN IMPORTANT BASIC INDUSTRY

In the seventeenth and eighteenth centuries, fishing was extremely important for New England's economy. Productive offshore ocean fishing banks and abundant supplies of shellfish made fishing "the cornerstone of New England's prosperity" for 150 years.[41]

The rapid growth of the region's economy soon reduced the relative importance of fishing. As early as 1880, fishermen accounted for less than 1 per cent of the total labor force. In 1950 the number of fishermen was about the same as it had been in 1880, even though the region's total labor force had more than doubled.[42] Between 1950 and 1963, however, the number of fishermen in New England declined by almost one-third, as imports of frozen fish cut into domestic markets.[43]

Recent developments have brought hopes that New England's fishing and fish-processing industry would rapidly expand. United States per capita consumption of fish has been increasing during the last decade, and the 1964 Fishing Fleet Improvement Act is designed to make New England fishermen competitive with foreign suppliers. Nevertheless, the best available forecast is that New England's fishing industry will do no more than stabilize at its present employment level.[44] With only 10,000 full-time fishermen and 5,000 workers in seafood-processing plants, New England's fishing industry is relatively unimportant compared to the region's major industries.[45]

NEW ENGLAND PORTS

Although a region may have few natural resources and be far from the growing centers of population, it can prosper if it has unusually good port facilities. Large ports, such as the Port of New York, conduct international trade for the entire nation. At such locations, various modes of transportation interconnect and a variety of specialized services are provided for shippers, such as freight forwarding, brokerage services, warehousing, maintenance and operation of terminals, and banking and insurance services. In addition, manufacturers locate nearby to minimize the total cost of assembling a variety of raw materials and component parts and of shipping finished products to many markets.

The port-related manufacturing employment, in turn, has a multiplier impact on employment in government and in the service, financial, construction, and transportation industries. Port of New York authorities have estimated, for example, that their port furnishes the economic basis of existence for one of every four persons living in the New York metropolitan area.[46]

Historically, New England ports have played an important role in the region's economic development.[47] This was particularly true in the eighteenth and nineteenth centuries. As late as 1877, Boston was a more important port than the ports of Philadelphia and Baltimore combined. However, the operations of the Port of New York have dwarfed those of the Port of Boston for more than a hundred years. And in recent decades, activity in Philadelphia and Baltimore has increased much faster than in Boston, which is now outstripped by each of them in total tonnage.

The changing composition of international trade has also hurt Boston. In the latter part of the nineteenth century, large quantities of grain, cereals, and meat products moved through its port on their way to Europe. Agricultural trade has since fallen off, and manufactured products now predominate among United States exports. These products are more likely to move through the ports of New York, Philadelphia, and Baltimore.

The Port of Boston's relative decline is explained mainly by the smaller hinterland served by the port. Other large ports along the eastern seaboard are served by railroads which provide direct long-haul freight service to the Midwest. Manufacturers in Connecticut are closer to New York, and even manufacturers in northern New England usually export through the Port of New York, which, because of its great size, offers better service and more frequent sailings. Altogether, about 85 per cent of the foreign exports from New England move through the New York port.[48]

Furthermore, Boston's general cargo trade is only about one-eighth the New York volume.[49] General cargo trade is important for the growth of a port city because it requires a large variety of auxiliary services, and thus has a large multiplier impact.

Boston is also disadvantaged because it is not a major last port of call. The last port of call is the most important one for exporters because it provides the fastest and most reliable service to foreign points. Goods loaded at earlier ports of call are more likely to be damaged by being handled repeatedly and are certain to be longer in transit. New York is the most important last port of call, as it has one great advantage: "No matter where you want to ship your goods, no matter when you want to ship them, New York is likely to have a ship leaving promptly thereafter for that destination."[50]

On the other hand, numerous ships do use Boston as a first port of call. This provides a delivery-time advantage to manufacturers who can buy raw materials or semifinished products from abroad.

New England consumers save when they buy imported products such as meat, wool manufactures, canned vegetables, tools and hardware, and liquors and wines, which are imported into Boston in substantial quantities.[51] The port also enables manufacturers to buy a large variety of raw materials and semifinished goods in world markets. Important products are wool, hides and skins, rubber, sugar, salt, molasses, lumber and logs, wood pulp, gypsum, semifinished and finished iron and steel, and industrial chemicals. Thus, imports partially offset the dearth of raw materials available within the New England region.

Conclusions

The evidence shows that New England has many locational disadvantages. The rapidly growing consumer markets are far distant. Fuel costs, power costs, living costs, the cost of most raw materials, construction costs, the poor quality of the soil, the weather, the tax structure, and port facilities all make it difficult to compete with producers located in more favored areas.

The region does have attractive vacation features. Some raw materials can be imported at a cost advantage. Petroleum products are available at below national average prices. And manufacturers do have easy access to the rich Middle Atlantic consumer and industrial markets. With the exception of scenery, however, New England has no unique advantage. Most states located along the Atlantic seaboard have similar industrial attractions, and many of these states do not have New England's locational disadvantages.

Chapter III

WAGES, SALARIES, AND INCOME IN NEW ENGLAND

Low Wages in New England

C HAPTER II demonstrated that during the twentieth century New England manufacturers have become increasingly burdened with geographical handicaps. This chapter will show that during most of this period New England manufacturing wages have been declining in relation to those in the nation. Now, most of the region's manufacturing employers have the advantage of paying below national average wages.

There are exceptions. For example, employers in four of New England's traditional industries—apparel, shoes and leather, textiles, and furniture—pay above national average wages. Furthermore, their wage-cost *dis*advantage has been increasing.

Generally, those firms in the region which pay wage rates above the national average for their industry are in industries that hire predominantly unskilled and semiskilled labor; those paying below industry average wages are usually in metalworking or research-oriented industries which require large numbers of professional, technical, and skilled employees.

Within New England, relative wage rates are typically highest in large metropolitan areas in southern New England and lowest in the smaller labor markets in northern New England. However, a few metropolitan areas in southern New England—Fall River, New Bedford, and Providence—have a low level of wages.

This chapter also explains how it is possible for a region with low manufacturing wages to have a very high level of per capita income.

MEASURING WAGE RATES AND WAGE COSTS

The term "wage" is subject to varying interpretations. The wage may be considered the amount earned per hour, per week, or per month. It may or may not include amounts put into retirement funds or paid for vacations and other fringe benefits. In the following pages, most wage-rate comparisons will be based on hourly earnings, including overtime pay but excluding fringe benefits. Data limitations generally preclude a broader study.[1]

Of course, wage-rate data do not always provide a reliable indicator of wage costs. In many underdeveloped countries, for example, wage rates are very low, but wage costs are high because efficient and dependable labor is unavailable.

It is probable, however, that in New England relatively low manufacturing wage rates are a good indicator of low wage costs. In 1949 the Federal Reserve Bank of Boston surveyed a large number of manufacturers in New England about their competitive advantages and disadvantages.[2] Most of the 663 respondents believed that the availability of labor and the "character" of the region's labor force offered them important advantages. In this survey the term "character" referred to dependability, productivity, and turnover. The availability of labor was thought to be an important advantage by 51 per cent of the respondents. The character of the labor force was considered an important attraction by 57 per cent. Less than 10 per cent thought either factor was a significant disadvantage.

Similarly, the 1954 report of the Committee of New England of the National Planning Association stated that New England workers transfer from one job to another less frequently than workers in other regions.[3] The report concluded that this was a significant advantage for New England firms.

The Federal Reserve Bank of Boston survey and the Committee of New England report both suggest that wage costs in New England are somewhat lower than the wage-rate statistics indicate. On the other hand, a study by Miernyk and Bright[4] indicates that most New England textile manufacturers believe that their competitors in other regions assign larger work loads. Studies by Lester[5] and Segal[6] suggest that there is no difference among regions of the United States in the efficiency of unskilled and semiskilled labor. Segal states that the differences in labor efficiency which do exist are likely to become progressively less important.[7]

The writer's opinion is that New England firms with high skill requirements have a somewhat greater wage-cost advantage than the wage-rate statistics indicate. At the same time, New England firms in the textile industry may have a slightly greater cost disadvantage than the wage-rate statistics suggest. Reliable wage-cost data are unavailable, however, and subsequent analyses are based entirely on wage-rate information.

THE HISTORICAL RECORD OF MANUFACTURING WAGE LEVELS

1869–1947. In 1869 annual manufacturing earnings per wage earner in New England were 5 per cent above the national average. Table 1 shows that the relative wage position of New England workers

TABLE 1

Total Wages per Wage Earner in Manufacturing Establishments in the New England States Relative to the United States Average, 1869–1947

Relative wages per wage earner: United States = 100

Area	1869	1889	1909	1929	1947
Maine	78	75	91	81	87
New Hampshire	90	84	89	83	86
Vermont	91	88	100	94	87
Massachusetts	110	104	100	95	96
Rhode Island	102	93	95	88	92
Connecticut	115	108	102	100	105
NEW ENGLAND	105	99	98	94	97

SOURCES: Everett S. Lee *et al., Population Redistribution and Economic Growth: United States, 1870–1950.* Vol. I. *Methodological Considerations and Reference Tables* (Philadelphia: The American Philosophical Society, 1957), Reference Table M–2, p. 684.

Simon Kuznets, Ann Ratner Miller, and Richard A. Easterlin, *Population Redistribution and Economic Growth: United States, 1870–1950.* Vol. II. *Analyses of Economic Change* (Philadelphia: The American Philosophical Society, 1960), Table A3.5, p. 129.

steadily declined between 1869 and the start of the depression in 1929. However, annual earnings per worker rose faster in the region than in the United States during and immediately after World War II, when most of the region's manufacturing capacity was being fully utilized.

1947–1964. Two sources of wage information are available for New England–United States comparisons during this period. Table 2

TABLE 2

New England–United States Average Hourly Wage Differentials for Production Workers in Manufacturing, 1950, 1960, and 1964

Industry	1950		1960		1964	
	Wage Differential between New England and the United States (1950 dollars)	New England Wages as a Percentage of United States Wages	Wage Differential between New England and the United States (1950 dollars)	New England Wages as a Percentage of United States Wages	Wage Differential between New England and the United States (1950 dollars)	New England Wages as a Percentage of United States Wages
MANUFACTURING	$−.11	92.5	$−.16	91.3	$−.13	93.4
DURABLE GOODS	−.12	92.2	−.14	92.6	−.16	92.5
Ordnance	−.02	98.7	−.25	88.3	−.34	85.5
Lumber & Wood	−.30	77.8	−.36	78.3	−.21	87.2
Furniture & Fixtures	−.02	98.4	+.03	101.6	+.02	101.3
Stone, Clay, Glass	+.11	107.6	+.03	101.3	+.06	103.1
Primary Metals	−.04	97.6	−.31	86.6	−.29	88.0
Fabricated Metal Products	−.16	89.6	−.24	87.8	−.19	90.8
Machinery (except electrical)	−.10	93.8	−.16	92.6	−.12	94.6
Electrical Machinery	−.12	91.9	−.21	88.7	−.15	92.3
Transportation Equipment	−.12	93.1	−.07	96.7	−.12	95.0
Instruments	−.15	89.9	−.19	90.3	−.16	91.9
NONDURABLE GOODS	−.08	94.2	−.12	92.8	−.09	94.9
Food & Kindred Products	−.10	92.6	−.15	91.8	−.09	95.1

TABLE 2 (*continued*)

Industry	1950		1960		1964	
	Wage Differential between New England and the United States (1950 dollars)	New England Wages as a Percentage of United States Wages	Wage Differential between New England and the United States (1950 dollars)	New England Wages as a Percentage of United States Wages	Wage Differential between New England and the United States (1950 dollars)	New England Wages as a Percentage of United States Wages
Textile-Mill Products	$+.07	105.6	$+.08	106.2	$+.08	105.8
Apparel	−.09	92.5	+.03	102.6	+.01	100.7
Paper & Pulp	−.09	93.6	−.12	93.4	−.08	96.0
Printing & Publishing	−.16	91.5	−.16	92.8	−.09	96.1
Chemicals	−.03	98.0	−.07	96.4	−.06	97.2
Rubber Products	−.22	86.1	−.23	88.9	−.12	93.9
Leather	+.06	105.1	+.08	106.1	+.07	105.0
Miscellaneous Manufactures	−.11	91.7	−.15	90.3	.00	100.0

SOURCE: Ronald C. Buehner, "The Effect of Walsh-Healey Minimum Wages on Regional Industries" (unpublished Master's thesis, School of Industrial Management, Massachusetts Institute of Technology, 1962), Appendix B.

U.S. Bureau of Labor Statistics, *Monthly Report on the Labor Force* (December, 1965), p. 45.

——, *Employment and Earnings Statistics for States and Areas: 1939–64* (Bulletin No. 1370–2) (Washington, D.C.: U.S. Government Printing Office, June, 1965).

——, *Consumer Price Index—U.S.: All Items, 1913 Forward—Series A (1957–59 = 100)* (Washington, D.C.: The Bureau [1962 release]).

——, *The Consumer Price Index, October 1965: U.S. City Average and Selected Areas* (Washington, D.C.: The Bureau [November 30, 1965 release]), Table A–7, p. 8.

Unpublished data furnished by U.S. Bureau of Labor Statistics, New England Regional Office, Boston, Mass., and by State Divisions of Employment Security presents weighted hourly wage comparisons (in 1950 dollars) based on employment and earnings data collected by the U.S. Bureau of Labor Statistics and state divisions of employment security. These comparisons originally were developed by Ronald C. Buehner at the Massachusetts Institute of Technology.[8] This information for the years 1950, 1960, and 1964 covers production workers, but excludes all salaried employees. Table 3 presents wage comparisons based on Census of Manufactures statistics for the years 1947, 1954, 1958, and 1963. These data include salaried workers, who are assumed to work 2,000 hours a year.

Census data for the years up through 1958 clearly show a continuation of the historical trend of declining relative wages in New England. The average manufacturing wage declined from 95.7 per cent of the national average in 1947 to 93.0 per cent in 1954 and 92.3 per cent in 1958. Employment and earnings data in Table 2 show a decline from 92.5 per cent in 1950 to 91.3 per cent in 1960.

Both sets of data show a reversal of the historical trend of regional manufacturing wages after about 1960. The census data show a rise from 92.3 per cent of the national average in 1958 to 93.9 per cent in 1963. Employment and earnings statistics indicate a rise from 91.3 per cent in 1960 to 93.4 per cent in 1964. As will be explained in Chapters IV and V, this reversal of trend was associated with a decline in unemployment in New England.

WAGE RATES BY INDUSTRY

The previous section has analyzed the trend of regional "average" manufacturing wages in New England. However, the real question is whether regional averages should be compared. Different regions and labor markets have different industrial compositions and skill requirements. A manufacturer comparing labor costs in different areas wants to know the relative cost of hiring labor in his particular industry, and not labor costs for all manufacturing.

In Table 3, New England–United States wage comparisons are shown before and after the national data are adjusted for New England's industrial composition. The adjustment is accomplished by assigning New England employment weights to the national average wage in each four-digit industry. The resulting adjusted average, computed for each two-digit industry and for manufacturing as a whole,

TABLE 3

Average Hourly Wage per Employee Man-Hour:ᵃ New England, United States Unadjusted, and United States Adjusted for New England's Industrial Composition

1947, 1954, 1958, and 1963

SIC Codeᵇ	Industry	Year	New England Average Hourly Wage per Employee Man-Hour	United States Unadjusted Average Hourly Wage per Employee Man-Hour	United States Adjusted Average Hourly Wage per Employee Man-Hour	New England Hourly Wage ÷ United States Unadjusted Hourly Wage	New England Hourly Wage ÷ United States Adjusted Hourly Wage	United States Unadjusted Hourly Wage ÷ United States Adjusted Hourly Wage
	ALL MFG.	1947	$1.310	$1.369	$1.342	95.7%	97.6%	102.0%
		1954	1.887	2.029	1.963	93.0	96.1	103.4
		1958	2.260	2.448	2.344	92.3	96.4	104.4
		1963	2.689	2.863	2.777	93.9	96.8	103.1
20	Food	1947	1.224	1.243	1.242	98.5	98.6	100.1
		1954	1.769	1.855	1.834	95.4	96.5	101.1
		1958	2.098	2.212	2.160	94.8	97.1	102.4
		1963	2.462	2.600	2.555	94.7	96.4	101.8
22	Textiles	1947	1.236	1.143	1.205	108.1	102.6	94.9
		1954	1.685	1.516	1.617	111.1	104.2	93.8
		1958	1.824	1.679	1.794	108.6	101.7	93.6
		1963	2.107	1.941	2.081	108.6	101.2	93.3

See footnotes at end of table.

SIC Code[b]	Industry	Year	New England Average Hourly Wage per Employee Man-Hour	United States Unadjusted Average Hourly Wage per Employee Man-Hour	United States Adjusted Average Hourly Wage per Employee Man-Hour	New England Hourly Wage ÷ United States Unadjusted Hourly Wage	New England Hourly Wage ÷ United States Adjusted Hourly Wage	United States Unadjusted Hourly Wage ÷ United States Adjusted Hourly Wage
23	Apparel	1947	$1.163	$1.266	$1.247	91.9%	93.3%	101.5%
		1954	1.431	1.496	1.526	95.7	93.8	98.0
		1958	1.668	1.696	1.755	98.3	95.0	96.6
		1963	1.920	1.890	1.942	101.6	98.9	97.3
24	Lumber	1947	1.009	1.033	1.040	97.7	97.0	99.3
		1954	1.293	1.563	1.554	82.7	83.2	100.6
		1958	1.666	1.792	1.834	93.0	90.8	97.7
		1963	1.905	2.107	2.101	90.4	90.7	100.3
25	Furniture	1947	1.214	1.214	1.231	100.0	98.6	98.6
		1954	1.728	1.750	1.736	98.7	99.5	100.8
		1958	2.020	2.025	1.996	99.8	101.2	101.5
		1963	2.291	2.263	2.254	101.2	101.6	100.4
26	Paper	1947	1.272	1.316	1.330	96.7	95.6	98.9
		1954	1.894	2.000	2.027	94.7	93.4	98.7
		1958	2.372	2.421	2.457	98.0	96.5	98.5
		1963	2.729	2.854	2.884	95.6	94.6	99.0
27	Printing	1947	1.455	1.578	1.558	92.2	93.4	101.3
		1954	2.121	2.308	2.256	91.9	94.0	102.3
		1958	2.524	2.695	2.655	93.7	95.1	101.5
		1963	2.866	3.081	3.047	93.0	94.1	101.1

See footnotes at end of table.

TABLE 3 (continued)

SIC Code[b]	Industry	Year	New England Average Hourly Wage per Employee Man-Hour	United States Unadjusted Average Hourly Wage per Employee Man-Hour	United States Adjusted Average Hourly Wage per Employee Man-Hour	New England Hourly Wage ÷ United States Unadjusted Hourly Wage	New England Hourly Wage ÷ United States Adjusted Hourly Wage	United States Unadjusted Hourly Wage ÷ United States Adjusted Hourly Wage
28	Chemicals	1947	$1.473	$1.479	$1.471	99.6%	100.1%	100.5%
		1954	2.229	2.320	2.324	96.1	95.9	99.8
		1958	2.668	2.818	2.842	94.7	93.9	99.2
		1963	3.191	3.336	3.333	95.7	95.7	100.1
30	Rubber	1947	1.320	1.524	1.392	86.6	94.8	109.5
		1954	2.028	2.216	2.041	91.5	99.4	108.6
		1958	2.293	2.513	2.374	91.2	96.6	105.9
		1963	2.630	2.845	2.655	92.4	99.1	107.2
31	Leather	1947	1.207	1.175	1.169	102.7	103.3	100.5
		1954	1.616	1.569	1.557	103.0	103.8	100.8
		1958	1.861	1.779	1.773	104.6	105.0	100.3
		1963	2.115	2.002	2.002	105.6	105.6	100.0
32	Stone	1947	1.415	1.237	1.395	114.4	101.4	88.7
		1954	1.981	1.942	2.023	102.0	97.9	96.0
		1958	2.457	2.358	2.376	104.2	103.4	99.2
		1963	2.890	2.757	2.782	104.8	103.9	99.1
33	Primary Metals	1947	1.463	1.545	1.524	94.7	96.0	101.4
		1954	2.223	2.362	2.354	94.1	94.4	100.3
		1958	2.647	3.008	2.773	88.0	95.5	108.5
		1963	2.984	3.441	3.163	86.7	94.3	108.8

TABLE 3 (continued)

SIC Code[b]	Industry	Year	New England Average Hourly Wage per Employee Man-Hour	United States Unadjusted Average Hourly Wage per Employee Man-Hour	United States Adjusted Average Hourly Wage per Employee Man-Hour	New England Hourly Wage ÷ United States Unadjusted Hourly Wage	New England Hourly Wage ÷ United States Adjusted Hourly Wage	United States Unadjusted Hourly Wage ÷ United States Adjusted Hourly Wage
34	Fabricated Metals	1947	$1.345	$1.424	$1.413	94.5%	95.2%	100.8%
		1954	1.976	2.147	2.110	92.0	93.6	101.8
		1958	2.388	2.583	2.525	92.5	94.6	102.3
		1963	2.714	2.906	2.864	93.4	94.8	101.5
35	Machinery (except elec.)	1947	1.463	1.492	1.508	98.1	97.0	98.9
		1954	2.179	2.311	2.292	94.3	95.1	100.8
		1958	2.572	2.766	2.708	93.0	95.0	102.1
		1963	3.103	3.212	3.182	96.6	97.5	100.9
36	Electrical Machinery	1947	1.315	1.409	1.371	93.3	95.9	102.8
		1954	1.882	2.083	2.045	90.4	92.0	101.9
		1958	2.312	2.554	2.487	90.5	93.0	102.7
		1963	2.896	3.079	3.018	94.1	96.0	102.0
37	Transportation Equipment	1947	1.489	1.576	1.578	94.5	94.4	99.9
		1954	2.269	2.391	2.363	94.9	96.0	101.2
		1958	2.745	2.942	2.962	93.3	92.7	99.3
		1963	3.393	3.484	3.585	97.4	94.6	97.2
38	Instruments	1947	1.334	1.421	1.413	93.9	94.4	100.6
		1954	1.972	2.201	2.105	89.6	93.7	104.6
		1958	2.352	2.719	2.561	86.5	91.8	106.2
		1963	2.893	3.132	3.014	92.4	96.0	103.9

See footnotes at end of table.

TABLE 3 (continued)

SIC Code[b]	Industry	Year	New England Average Hourly Wage per Employee Man-Hour	United States Unadjusted Average Hourly Wage per Employee Man-Hour	United States Adjusted Average Hourly Wage per Employee Man-Hour	New England Hourly Wage ÷ United States Unadjusted Hourly Wage	New England Hourly Wage ÷ United States Adjusted Hourly Wage	United States Unadjusted Hourly Wage ÷ United States Adjusted Hourly Wage
39	Misc.	1947	$1.227	$1.265	$1.278	97.0%	96.0%	99.0%
		1954	1.709	1.780	1.745	96.0	97.9	102.0
		1958	2.002	2.081	2.035	96.2	98.4	102.3
		1963	2.349	2.370	2.328	99.1	100.9	101.8

[a] Man-hours include estimated figures for salaried employees, who are assumed to work 2,000 hours a year.

[b] In 1947 and 1954 four-digit industries were classified according to definitions in the 1945 edition of the Standard Industrial Classification Code. In 1958 and 1963 industry definitions were from the revised 1957 edition of the code. Although totals for all manufacturing are affected only slightly by the changes in code, some two-digit industry groups in 1958 and 1963 are not strictly comparable with those in the earlier years.

SOURCES: U.S. Bureau of the Census, *Census of Manufactures: 1947* (Washington, D.C.: U.S. Government Printing Office, 1949–1950).

————, *U.S. Census of Manufactures: 1954* (Washington, D.C.: U.S. Government Printing Office, 1957).

————, *U.S. Census of Manufactures: 1958* (Preliminary Reports Series MC[P]) (Washington, D.C.: U.S. Government Printing Office, 1959–1960).

————, *U.S. Census of Manufactures: 1958* (Washington, D.C.: U.S. Government Printing Office, 1961).

————, *Census of Manufactures: 1963* (Preliminary Reports Series MC63[P]) (Washington, D.C.: U.S. Government Printing Office, 1965).

————, *Census of Manufactures: 1963* (Industry Statistics Preprints Series MC63[2]) (Washington, D.C.: U.S. Government Printing Office, 1966).

shows what the national average would be if the United States had the same industrial composition as New England.

The adjustment process is not perfect. In some industries, such as paper and allied products, a good adjustment is impossible. About 40 per cent of New England's output in this industry is concentrated in one subindustry: paper-mill operations. And paper-mill operations in New England are not at all comparable with similarly classified operations in the nation.

In general, however, the weighting process does work, and it shows that almost half of the New England–United States wage differential is accounted for by the concentration of New England manufacturing firms in low-wage industries. Nevertheless, the average manufacturing wage in New England is still significantly lower than the adjusted national average.

Both Tables 2 and 3 show that the relative wage varies considerably from industry to industry in New England. Four of New England's traditional industries—textiles, leather and shoes, furniture, and apparel—pay above national average wages. Even though the average wage in all manufacturing in New England was declining in relation to the national average between 1947 and 1958, the regional average wage in these four industries was increasing faster than in the nation.

This is somewhat surprising, because these are stable or contracting industries and generally are not highly profitable in New England. However, these industries use a large amount of unskilled and semi-skilled labor, which is becoming increasingly scarce in the region. Since 1920, federal immigration laws have discriminated against unskilled workers moving in from other countries. Unlike the South, the Midwest, and the Lake states, New England no longer has a substantial rural population moving into its cities.[9] Furthermore, these traditional industries have difficulty in competing for labor with the rapidly growing metalworking industries in New England. Although these growth industries pay below national average wage rates in their industries, their pay scales are higher for most categories of labor than those in the textile, shoe and leather, apparel, and furniture industries.

OCCUPATIONAL WAGE RATES BY METROPOLITAN AREA

The adjusted census wage statistics in the previous section provide a comparison of the average level of New England manufacturing wages with the level of wages in the same group of industries in the United States. This information has theoretical interest and is useful to employers. Employees, however, wish to compare wage levels for specific jobs in labor markets across the country. Occupational-earnings studies of the Bureau of Labor Statistics provide such information,[10] much of which is summarized in Appendix A. These studies show that some skilled male manufacturing workers (such as machine-tool operators, millwrights, and sheet-metal workers) receive lower wages in New England than in any other region of the country. Among large cities, Providence, Rhode Island, has the lowest wage rates for skilled labor.

Semiskilled male manufacturing workers are paid lower wages in New England than in the Middle Atlantic, North Central, and western states. Southern cities, however, generally pay the lowest wages for this type of labor. Unskilled male manufacturing workers in New England usually receive wage rates somewhat below the national average. Again, the lowest wage rates are in southern cities. Wage rates for women office workers in New England manufacturing plants are generally well below the national average and below those prevailing in southern states.

The Bureau of Labor Statistics also publishes an index of the average wage for twenty-nine key jobs based on a survey of eighty metropolitan areas throughout the United States and projected for all Standard Metropolitan Statistical Areas. The information for the listed New England cities is shown in Table 4. The list of twenty-nine key jobs is shown in Table 5.

This wage-level information for manufacturing workers is deficient in that it excludes production workers. Nonetheless, Table 4 clearly indicates that average manufacturing wages for specific jobs are relatively low in New England.

A SPECIAL SURVEY OF THE METALWORKING INDUSTRIES

Of particular importance to the region is that relatively low wages prevail in the region's growing manufacturing industries, enabling them to prosper. In the postwar period the metalworking industries have been the fast-growing industries in New England. In a 1962 Ph.D. dissertation at the Massachusetts Institute of Technology, Pardee collected detailed information on the wage rates of various

TABLE 4

Interarea Pay Comparisons, New England and the United States

Relative pay levels by industry divisions, March 1963 through February 1964.
Pay levels for each industry and occupational group in all areas = 100.

New England Cities	Office Clerical			Skilled Maintenance		Unskilled Plant		
	All Industries	Mfg. Industries	Non-Mfg. Industries	All Industries	Mfg. Industries	All Industries	Mfg. Industries	Non-Mfg. Industries
AREAS WITH 1,000,000 OR MORE PEOPLE								
Boston	93	91	95	94	94	97	93	101
AREAS WITH 250,000–1,000,000 PEOPLE								
New Haven	99	95	101	90	91	94	96	93
Providence-Pawtucket	85	83	85	85	84	86	78	98
Worcester	92	91	86	90	90	96	89	98
AREAS WITH LESS THAN 250,000 PEOPLE								
Lawrence-Haverhill	91	—	—	88	89	91	87	97
Manchester (N.H.)	81	—	—	—	—	77	72	83
Portland (Me.)	84	—	85	81	81	86	88	82
Waterbury (Conn.)	99	95	—	91	90	99	100	91

SOURCE: U.S. Bureau of Labor Statistics, *Wages and Related Benefits. Part II. Metropolitan Areas, United States and Regional Summaries, 1963–64* (Bulletin No. 1385–82) (Washington, D.C.: U.S. Government Printing Office, 1965), Table 1, p. 68.

TABLE 5

Jobs Studied in Interarea Pay Comparison,
New England and the United States
March 1963–February 1964

Office Clerical Workers

Bookkeeping-machine operators, class B
Clerks, accounting, class A
Clerks, accounting, class B
Clerks, file, class A
Clerks, file, class B
Clerks, file, class C
Clerks, order
Clerks, payroll
Comptometer operators
Keypunch operators, class A
Keypunch operators, class B
Office boys and girls
Secretaries
Stenographers, general
Stenographers, senior
Switchboard operators
Tabulating-machine operators, class B
Typists, class A
Typists, class B

Skilled Men Maintenance Workers

Carpenters
Electricians
Machinists
Mechanics
Mechanics (automotive)
Painters
Pipefitters
Tool and die makers

Unskilled Men Plant Workers

Janitors, porters, and cleaners
Laborers, material handling

SOURCE: U.S. Bureau of Labor Statistics, *Wages and Related Benefits.* Part II. *Metropolitan Areas, United States and Regional Summaries, 1963–64* (Bulletin No. 1385–82) (Washington, D.C.: U.S. Government Printing Office, 1965), p. 72.

types of metalworking firms in twenty-six metropolitan areas throughout the United States.[11] He obtained data from personal interviews and from official sources for firms in the fabricated metal, instrument, machinery (except electrical), electrical machinery, and transportation equipment industries. He collected uniform statistics for eighteen key jobs which provided wage-rate data representative of almost all kinds of skills required by these industries. The skill distribution of different kinds of firms was estimated by analyzing the questionnaire returns of firms specializing in skilled and unskilled assembly operations and unskilled machine-tool operations.

By applying the average reported wage for each job in each city and adding up the number of persons employed in each job in each "typical" firm, Pardee obtained an estimate of the total wage bill for four different types of metalworking firms in each of twenty-six cities. The results, expressed in index numbers, are given in Table 6. They show that wage levels are considerably lower in the metalworking industries in cities in New England than in cities throughout the country. For example, the average wage in metropolitan Boston is usually 5 to 20 per cent lower than in other metropolitan areas throughout the country. An important exception is Dallas, Texas, where wage rates are 15 per cent lower than those in Boston.

Strictly speaking, it is unfair to compare New England cities, other than Boston, with the largest cities outside the region. If a very large manufacturing firm decided to move into some New England cities, it could change the whole wage structure with the impact of its own hiring. Small cities such as Manchester, New Hampshire, and Portland, Maine, have thin labor markets and a scarcity of suppliers of specialized services and materials. Specialized technicians are scarce, good secretaries are difficult to find, and few scientists and engineers are available locally.

However, if a firm wished to have a simple assembly operation using predominantly semiskilled workers, a northern New England location might bring savings of 4 to 8 per cent of total production costs as compared to Boston. Undoubtedly, lower labor costs are one of the major reasons that many electronic and other metalworking firms have chosen in recent years to place new plants in northern New England and in some of the older mill towns in southern New England.[12] During the postwar period, a large part of New England's shoe industry has migrated from southern New England to northern New England to take advantage of low-cost labor.[13]

TABLE 6

Set I Typical Firms in 26 United States Cities: Average Hourly Rate per Employee, 18 Jobs, 1960

As a percentage of Boston rate

City	Unskilled Assembly Operations	Skilled Assembly Operations	Skilled Machine Tool Operations	Unskilled Machine Tool Operations
Detroit	123	121	123	124
San Francisco–Oakland	120	117	119	122
Pittsburgh	119	117	117	119
Cleveland	116	112	112	115
Chicago	109	109	111	113
Portland, Oregon	121	112	113	117
Milwaukee	121	113	114	118
Los Angeles–Long Beach	99	105	107	107
Buffalo	112	105	104	111
St. Louis	105	105	111	110
New York City	102	102	102	102
Newark–Jersey City	105	104	105	107
Philadelphia	98	103	106	109
Denver	102	104	108	107
Houston	95	101	105	108
SPRINGFIELD–HOLYOKE	113	102	102	110
Baltimore	89	101	101	98
BOSTON	100	100	100	100
HARTFORD	99	100	102	109
Minneapolis–St. Paul	98	98	99	101
NEW HAVEN	94	98	99	103
WORCESTER	100	97	97	98
PROVIDENCE	90	95	98	98
PORTLAND, MAINE	81	88	91	90
Dallas	78	84	87	87
MANCHESTER, NEW HAMPSHIRE	76	75	78	79

SOURCE: Scott E. Pardee, "A Study of Inter-City Wage Differentials" (unpublished Ph.D. dissertation, Department of Economics and Social Science, Massachusetts Institute of Technology, 1962), p. 60.

Explaining New England's High Per Capita Personal Income

THE PARADOX

Previous sections have shown that manufacturing wages and salaries in New England in 1960 were 9 per cent lower than those in the nation. In many, if not most, occupations, earnings in manufacturing are as low as or lower than those prevailing in the Southeast.

On the other hand, per capita personal income payments in New England in 1960 were 11 per cent above the national average. This compares with a per capita personal income level in the Southeast which was more than 25 per cent below the national average.

Here is a paradox: manufacturing earnings are relatively low in New England, but the level of per capita personal income is high. The following factors explain most of this discrepancy.

SIX IMPORTANT FACTORS

1. *A larger proportion of the population in New England is employed.* In New England 39.4 per cent of the population are employed, while the average in the United States is only 37.0 per cent. Because relatively more people work in New England than in the United States, the earnings of the employed are divided among proportionately fewer dependents. In this way, low earning rates are converted into a high per capita personal income level. Table 7 (Adjustment 4) shows that about one-third of the discrepancy between New England's low average manufacturing earning rate (91 per cent of the national average) and New England's high per capita income (111 per cent of the national average) is explained by this one factor.[14]

Why do more people work in New England? First, a larger percentage of the population is of working age. Here 60.0 per cent of the population are between the ages of fifteen and sixty-four. This same age group constitutes 59.7 per cent of the population in the nation. Children under the age of fifteen constitute 31.1 per cent of the nation's population, but only 29.3 per cent of New England's.

Second, the labor-force participation rate is higher in New England than in the United States. In 1960, 57.1 per cent of the region's population aged fourteen and over were working. This compared to 55.3 per cent in the nation. The higher participation rate is largely explained by the greater proportion of working women in the region. Why do more women work in New England? It is probable that light

TABLE 7

New England–United States per Capita Personal Income Comparisons, 1960

Adjustment	New England 1960 Data Used	United States 1960 Data Used	New England 1960 Income Data Adjusted	United States 1960 Income Data Adjusted	New England 1960 Income Data as a Percentage of U.S. 1960 Income Data
Unadjusted total 1960 per capita income figures for the United States and New England.	population 4/60 personal income 1960	population 4/60 personal income 1960	$2,480 (unadjusted data)	$2,230 (unadjusted data)	111.2
(1) Total 1960 per capita income adjusted to exclude property income.	$366 (property income per capita)	$290 (property income per capita)	$2,114	$1,940	108.9
(2) Total 1960 per capita income adjusted to exclude property income *and* transfer payments minus personal contributions for social insurance.	$149 (transfer payments per capita minus per capita personal contributions for social insurance)	$110 (transfer payments per capita minus per capita personal contributions for social insurance)	$1,965	$1,830	107.4

TABLE 7 (continued)

Adjustment	New England 1960 Data Used	United States 1960 Data Used	New England 1960 Income Data Adjusted	United States 1960 Income Data Adjusted	New England 1960 Income Data as a Percentage of U.S. 1960 Income Data
(3) Total 1960 per capita income adjusted to exclude property income, transfer payments, and "other labor income." "Other labor income" includes employers' contributions to pension funds, compensation for injuries, pay of military reservists, and miscellaneous.	$65 ("other labor income" per capita)	$61 ("other labor income" per capita)	$1,900 (current earnings per capita)	$1,769 (current earnings per capita)	107.4
(4) Adjusting 1960 current earnings per capita to 1960 current earnings per person employed as of April 1960. Current earnings include proprietors' income and all wages and salaries.	39.4 (percentage of total population employed 4/60)	37.0 (percentage of total population employed 4/60)	$4,825 (current earnings per person employed)	$4,780 (current earnings per person employed)	100.9

TABLE 7 · (continued)

Adjustment	New England 1960 Data Used	United States 1960 Data Used	New England 1960 Income Data Adjusted	United States 1960 Income Data Adjusted	New England 1960 Income Data as a Percentage of U.S. 1960 Income Data
(5) Adjusting U.S. composition of economic activity to that prevailing in New England.	See Table B–5	See Table B–5	$4,825	$4,807	100.4
(6) Adjusting employment data for April seasonal variation.	98.7 (seasonal factor for April)	99.3 (seasonal factor for April)	$4,762	$4,774	99.8

Sources: Robert E. Graham, Jr., and Edwin J. Coleman, "Consumer Incomes Up in All Regions in 1960," *Survey of Current Business*, XLI (August, 1961), 14–15.

U.S. Bureau of the Census, *U.S. Census of Population: 1960*. Vol. I. *Characteristics of the Population*. Part I. *United States Summary*. (Washington, D.C.: U.S. Government Printing Office, 1964), Tables 105 and 119.

Table B–5, Appendix B in this volume.

industry and a diversified economy offer more job opportunities for women. It may also be that more wives work because their husbands' earnings are relatively low.[15]

Third, when the last Decennial Census was taken in 1960, fewer persons in New England were receiving reduced income because of unemployment. In April of that year New England's unemployment rate (as a percentage of the civilian labor force) was 4.6 per cent. This compared with 5.1 per cent for the nation.[16]

2. *Per capita property income is greater in New England than in the United States.* In 1960 per capita property income payments amounted to $366 in New England and only $290 in the nation. Greater property income is largely explained by more inherited wealth and by greater per capita saving made possible by higher income levels. Table 7 (Adjustment 1) shows that property income accounts for an important part of the differential between New England's low manufacturing earning rates and its high per capita personal income.

3. *Per capita transfer payments are greater in New England than in the United States.* In New England, as of 1960, per capita transfer payments (minus per capita personal contributions to social insurance) amounted to $149. In the United States the figure was $110 (Table 7, Adjustment 2).

This difference is explained by several factors. Proportionately more older people receive Old Age and Survivors Insurance benefits in New England than in the nation. A larger portion of the region's population is sixty-five years of age and over and, historically, a larger portion of the population has had social insurance coverage. In addition, public assistance payments tend to be slightly more generous in New England than in other parts of the country.

The inclusion of public assistance and veterans' payments in the personal income statistics for each state involves double counting. These payments are financed by tax receipts, most of which in turn are paid from wage and salary payments and other income of individuals already included in the personal income totals.

4. *Per capita "other labor income" is slightly greater in New England than in the United States.* "Other labor income" includes employers' contributions to private pension and welfare funds, compensation for injuries, the pay of military reservists, and miscellaneous other income (Table 7, Adjustment 3).

5. *New England has a favorable composition of economic activity.* When average earnings per person in each sector of the United States economy are weighted to reflect New England's greater concentration of employment in certain major sectors (for instance, a high percentage in manufacturing, a low percentage in agriculture), the resulting United States weighted earnings are higher than unweighted earnings (Table 7, Adjustment 5).

6. *The seasonal pattern of employment variation in New England differs from that in the United States.* The Decennial Census was taken in April 1960; in April, United States employment amounts to about 99.3 per cent of its yearly average. In New England the seasonal factor for April is 98.7. When adjustment is made and the employment figures are increased to account for these seasonality differences, United States earnings per person employed are higher relative to those in New England (Table 7, Adjustment 6).

OTHER CONTRIBUTING FACTORS

Table 7 still leaves questions unanswered. It suggests that, after adjustment, current earnings per person employed in all types of economic activity in 1960 were roughly the same in New England as in the United States. On the other hand, this chapter has demonstrated conclusively that wages and salaries in manufacturing have been considerably lower in New England than in the United States.

Table 4 shows that some of this difference can be explained by the fact that New England nonmanufacturing wage rates are closer to those prevailing in the United States than are manufacturing wage rates. As shown in Appendix B, this appears to be true in almost all kinds of nonmanufacturing work.

Furthermore, Table 8 suggests that the labor force in New England has a slightly higher occupational skill level than that in the nation. It would be logical, therefore, that earnings per person employed, shown in Adjustment 6 of Table 7, would be higher relative to those in the nation than would wage rates in particular occupations shown in Table 4.

Some of the remaining discrepancy between Table 7 and Table 4 may be attributable to a greater proportion of multiple-job holders in New England. If an employee has two or more jobs, his total earnings are included in the personal income statistics. However, the Decennial

TABLE 8

*Occupational Distribution of Wage and Salaried Workers
in All Industries Excluding Agriculture, Forestry,
and Fishing in New England and the United States,
1960*

Classification of Occupations	New England (Percentage of Employment)	United States (Percentage of Employment)
Professional	12.4	12.2
Technicians	1.0	.9
Managerial[a]	5.9	6.1
Craftsmen	16.3	15.8
Sales	7.8	8.4
Clerical	17.0	16.8
Bookkeepers	1.6	1.6
Cashiers	.7	.9
Operatives	25.0	21.4
Services	10.8	13.0
Charwomen, Janitors, Porters	1.2	1.7
Laborers	3.9	5.4
TOTAL	100.0[b]	100.0[b]

[a] Does not include self-employed.

[b] Detail may not add to total due to rounding.

SOURCES: U.S. Bureau of the Census, *U.S. Census of Population: 1960. Detailed Characteristics.* Connecticut, Maine, Massachusetts, New Hampshire, Rhode Island, and Vermont (separate publication for each state) (Series PC[1]) (Washington, D.C.: U.S. Government Printing Office, 1962), Table 125.

————, *U.S. Census of Population: 1960. Supplementary Reports. Industry Group by Occupation: 1960* (Series PC[S1]–27) (Washington, D.C.: U.S. Government Printing Office, 1962).

Census tabulates an employee only in his primary job. Thus, earnings per person employed provide an estimate of earnings per job that is biased upward. This bias is probably more serious in New England than in the United States.

The region's earnings data shown in Table 7 are also biased upward because of the inclusion of Fairfield County, Connecticut. The residents of this county are largely dependent on income earned in New York City and do not belong in a New England economic region. The tables in Appendix B show that their earnings are much higher than those of other residents of New England.

Chapter IV

WAGE THEORY

CHAPTER III demonstrated that during the twentieth century most manufacturing wage rates in New England have been below those in the nation. Furthermore, until about 1960, the region's average manufacturing wage showed no long-run tendency to move toward the national average.

Why do wage rates differ among regions and areas in an integrated national economy? Many economists emphasize traditional supply-demand analysis and the importance of labor immobility. Others believe that differences in industrial composition determine interregional and interarea wage differentials. This chapter will compare and analyze the ideas of both groups of economists.

Explanations of Interarea Wage Differentials

THE CLASSICAL EXPLANATION

Wage differentials have traditionally been explained by local variations in the supply of and demand for labor. Wage rates would be low in poorly endowed areas where employers cannot afford to pay high wages and in areas where employment is declining or growing slowly and the work force is increasing rapidly. Wage rates would be high in favorably situated areas where labor is scarce.

The traditional classical view has also been that interregional and interarea differentials would gradually decline in national economies where employers and employees are free to migrate. According to this theory, the only differentials which should exist in the long run would be those traceable to area differences in the cost of living or to the cost of moving from low-wage to high-wage areas.

Nevertheless, wage rates in a number of areas of the country have shown little long-run tendency to converge to national levels. Chapter

III showed that wages in New England manufacturing declined in relation to the national average from 1889 through 1929 and again between 1947 and 1958. Wage rates have been very low in the South for a hundred years. Bloch has demonstrated that in the South relative manufacturing wage levels were about the same in 1945–1946 as they were in 1917.[1] Segal has shown that there was only a slight trend toward convergence in the South in the prosperous years between 1947 and 1954.[2]

Economists sympathetic to the classical theory of area wage differentials generally attribute the lack of convergence to labor immobility or to national unemployment problems. They point to studies which show sluggish migration from depressed areas during boom periods and migration to low-income rural areas during recessions. Carter Goodrich has shown that the Southern Appalachian Coal Plateau area, one of the lowest-income areas in the United States, had a population gain of 18 per cent in the prosperous decade between 1920 and 1930.[3] Although 43 of the 66 coal-plateau counties for which data were available had migration losses in the twenties, only 18 had population declines and 15 of these had population losses of less than 10 per cent. In most of these counties, out-migration was overwhelmed by the natural population increase.

Goodrich and other members of the Population Redistribution Study also demonstrated that during the depression of the thirties there was a reflux of migration to low-income counties in the Southern Appalachian Coal Plateau, in the southeastern states, and in the Cutover region of northern Minnesota, Wisconsin, and Michigan. Rather than be unemployed in a high-wage urban area, these migrants preferred to eke out an existence on substandard farms.

It can be argued that these depression conditions were very unusual. Furthermore, the Southern Appalachian Coal Plateau has long been known for poverty, high birth rates, poor education, and a sense of isolation. Other studies suggest, however, that sluggish migration occurs during prosperous periods in less isolated areas where average income and education levels are high and birth rates are low. Reynolds[4] and Miernyk[5] have shown that many unemployed experienced workers in New England cities have not considered looking for work in unfamiliar surroundings in other labor markets.

Thus the burden of migration falls on new entrants to the labor force and younger workers. However, many economists believe that most young people are unwilling to move long distances for wage differentials amounting to 10 or 20 per cent. Segal believes that mass migration—sufficient to reduce the labor supply of a low-wage area—occurs only in periods of great labor shortage.[6] Similarly, Sjaastad[7] has concluded that in most states in the United States per capita income would have to fall to a level 50 per cent below the national average before net out-migration would exceed the natural population increase.

In discussing interarea wage differentials, Duesenberry has developed a good summary of the modified classical theory based on labor immobility. He concludes that changes in relative wage levels in different labor markets (where unions are not dominant) occur because of "differences in the rates of growth of the industries located in those labor markets and, to some extent, because of differences in rates of natural increase." If the growth of jobs exceeds the growth of the labor force, the result is active bidding for the unattached workers. As the local wage level moves up, younger workers in other labor markets in the surrounding region are attracted by the availability of high-paying jobs. Thus, migration "tends to limit inter-area differentials but does not tend to eliminate them."[8]

THE INDUSTRIAL-COMPOSITION EXPLANATION

Implicit in Duesenberry's analysis is that varying unemployment levels determine the relative movement of wage levels in different labor markets. Other economists claim, however, that the composition of industry in each labor market determines the level and structure of manufacturing wage rates.[9] They point out that some industries pay high wages, wherever they are located; others pay low wages in all locations. Some firms have the financial ability to pay high wages; others can only afford low wages. Some firms are vulnerable to union pressure; others are not. Thus, if a community happens to have the kind of industries which have substantial market power, have a proportionately small total wage bill, and are vulnerable to union bargaining, that community will enjoy a high level of manufacturing wages. On the other hand, low wage levels would be expected in communities whose employers are in labor-intensive industries where there is severe competition in product markets. According to the industrial-composition theory, local unemployment conditions will generally have little influence on the level or trend of local or regional manufacturing wages.

Proponents of this theory can point to a variety of studies which suggest that the forces determining wages in local labor markets are somewhat different from those which influence prices in other markets. Ruggles[10] has shown, for example, that the cost of labor declined relatively slowly during the depression of the thirties. In this period, of course, almost every labor market had a large amount of unemployment. Slichter,[11] Reynolds,[12] Dunlop,[13] and Garbarino[14] all have demonstrated that certain industries generally pay substantially higher wages than others. These are usually capital-intensive industries which typically consist of large corporations with considerable market power. These firms have such power because entry into their industry is difficult or because a partial spatial monopoly exists. Generally they can afford to pay high wages. As a result they are more vulnerable to union bargaining than are firms which face serious competition in product markets.

Various studies have also shown that firms differ widely in the wage rates they pay for the same type of labor in the same labor market. In a study of selected occupations in sixty-three labor markets, Lester found that the average hourly earnings in the highest-paying establishments exceeded those in the lowest-paying plants in the same labor market by an average of 50 per cent.[15]

In his study of the New Haven labor market, Reynolds discovered that in 1948 the starting rate for unskilled labor in different plants ranged from a low of $.69 an hour to a high of $1.18 an hour.[16] The firms paying the highest wages were in capital-intensive industries such as steel and paper. Low wages prevailed in the garment industry, in small struggling firms in the metalworking industries, and in firms where labor costs accounted for 40 to 60 per cent of total costs.

Dunlop has reported on the variation in hourly earnings of truck drivers in the Boston labor market in 1951.[17] He compared the earnings of truck drivers employed by different types of firms in both manufacturing and nonmanufacturing. Although every firm in his sample was organized by the Teamsters Union, hourly rates ranged from a low of $1.20 for truckers hauling scrap iron and steel to a high of $2.25 for those transporting magazines. Dunlop concluded that these differentials could be attributed to numerous factors, but that major emphasis should be placed on differences in competitive conditions among employers. Those firms paying the highest wages benefit from an inelastic demand for their products and from the fact that wage payments make up a small fraction of total costs.

Walker has analyzed wage differentials in the Boston labor market in 1960 among thirty-eight large firms in finance, retail trade, manufacturing, and public utilities.[18] His study was unusual because he had access to confidential employer records enabling him to compare wage rates for specific clerical jobs which were similar in all respects. In his sample, many employers paid wage rates 25 per cent or more above those paid by others.

Economists who favor the industrial-composition theory claim that migration cannot eliminate intra- and interarea wage differentials. This point is supported by the fact that when workers observe an employer paying wage rates 30 per cent above the market, they do not attempt to replace an employee in a job by offering to work for a wage only 20 per cent above the market. Instead they simply wait for an opening to develop in the high-wage firm. In this respect labor markets differ from most other markets. Even when unemployed, most workers are unwilling to undercut the wage rates of other workers.

Proponents of the industrial-composition theory of interarea wage differentials point to certain labor markets where manufacturing wage rates are high and unemployment rates have also been high. For example, the average manufacturing wage in the Pittsburgh labor market moved up from 114.7 to 123.3 per cent of the national average between 1951 and 1961, despite a 27 per cent decline in manufacturing employment. Pittsburgh was an area with substantial unemployment for almost one-half this period. During these years Buffalo and Detroit also improved their wage standings, despite similar unemployment records. In 1961 the average manufacturing wage in Buffalo was 119.0 per cent and in Detroit 128.4 per cent of the national average.

Table 9 provides additional evidence that in these (and other) cities manufacturing wage rates are artificially high and that industrial composition is largely responsible. It shows that in Detroit, Buffalo, and Pittsburgh the average pay in 1963–1964 for selected jobs in nonmanufacturing establishments generally ranged between 80 and

TABLE 9

*Selected Job Category Pay Levels in Nonmanufacturing
as a Percentage of Manufacturing Pay in Same Area,
1963–1964*

Area	Office Clerical	Unskilled Plant
NEW ENGLAND		
Boston	95	102
Manchester	—	108
New Haven	97	91
Portland (Me.)	—	87
Providence	93	117
Worcester	87	103
MIDDLE ATLANTIC		
Albany–Schenectady–Troy	95	106
Allentown–Bethlehem–Easton	—	96
Buffalo	89	84
Newark and Jersey City	96	91
New York	94	99
Patterson–Clifton–Passaic	91	104
Philadelphia	92	95
Pittsburgh	85	91
Scranton	108	112
Trenton	—	98
York	—	108
SOUTH		
Atlanta	92	93
Baltimore	86	80
Beaumont–Port Arthur	—	75
Birmingham	84	73
Charlestown (W.Va.)	—	83
Charlotte	—	114
Chattanooga	91	81
Dallas	92	92
Fort Worth	83	73
Greenville	—	114
Houston	91	79
Jackson	—	96
Jacksonville	—	96
Little Rock–North Little Rock	—	94
Louisville	92	85

TABLE 9 (*continued*)

Area	Office Clerical	Unskilled Plant
Lubbock	—	104
Memphis	90	93
Miami	—	106
New Orleans	86	79
Norfolk–Portsmouth–Newport News–Hampton	—	72
Oklahoma City	94	101
Raleigh	—	106
Richmond	91	85
San Antonio	—	94
Savannah	—	94
Washington, D.C.	—	95
NORTH CENTRAL		
Akron	83	91
Canton	—	82
Chicago	97	103
Cincinnati	93	89
Cleveland	91	89
Columbus	87	87
Davenport–Rock Island–Moline	81	85
Dayton	91	81
Des Moines	90	81
Detroit	81	84
Green Bay	—	105
Indianapolis	84	83
Kansas City	95	87
Milwaukee	90	91
Minneapolis–St. Paul	100	99
Omaha	96	97
Rockford	—	108
St. Louis	95	91
South Bend	84	86
Toledo	92	95
Waterloo	—	84
Wichita	—	88
WEST		
Albuquerque	—	107
Boise	—	—
Denver	95	91

TABLE 9 (*continued*)

Area	Office Clerical	Unskilled Plant
Los Angeles–Long Beach	93	99
Phoenix	89	94
Portland (Ore.)	100	104
Salt Lake City	93	95
San Bernardino–Riverside–Ontario	—	83
San Francisco–Oakland	93	100
Seattle	87	100
Spokane	—	89

SOURCE: Unpublished data furnished by U.S. Bureau of Labor Statistics, Division of Occupational Pay.

90 per cent of the average pay for the identical jobs in manufacturing establishments. This dual wage structure is clearly not compatible with the classical theory.

In these areas, high manufacturing wage rates are probably the result of union bargaining with large multiplant firms on a nationwide basis, of the proportionately small share of labor costs in the cost structure of the dominant employers, and of the market power of these employers. In these labor markets, high wage rates are probably not the result of tight labor markets.[19] Instead, high wage rates may bring high rates of unemployment.[20] Even if local unemployment were substantial, most large employers in the metalworking industries in Detroit would have great difficulty with unions and workers if they attempted to pay below industry average wages. On the other hand, many nonmanufacturing employers, whose wage structures generally are not directly compared with those of manufacturing firms, are able to retain a labor force at relatively low rates of pay.

This does not mean that high unemployment rates have no influence on manufacturing wage rates in cities where heavy industry accounts for most of the employment. Wage rates throughout the country move up much more slowly when there is substantial unemployment.[21] However, unemployment has less influence, and other factors such as unions play a more significant role, in local labor markets where certain types of capital-intensive industries predominate.

Attempts at Statistical Measurement of the Importance of Industrial Composition

Both the classical and the industrial-composition theories are logical, and both appear to provide a partial explanation of interarea wage differentials. Most economists are willing to admit that some industries have almost identical wage structures in all labor markets and that wage rates in other industries are determined by local supply-and-demand situations.[22] The unanswered question is: Which theory does the better job of explaining interarea wage differentials in most labor markets in the United States?

Because many industries appear to pay high (or low) wages, wherever they are located, a number of researchers have attempted to estimate what portion of interarea wage differentials can be "explained" by industrial composition and how much by other factors. To accomplish this, Pardee has correlated average manufacturing earnings in sixty-one labor markets with "industry weighted earnings" in these same labor markets.[23] He used a simple estimating equation of the form:

$$W_j = a + bI_j$$

where $W_j =$ the actual manufacturing wage in the jth labor market and $I_j =$ "industry weighted earnings." This is what the average manufacturing wage in the jth labor market would be if each firm in the jth labor market paid the national average wage in its industry. Pardee analyzed his industries on a two- and sometimes a three-digit basis.

Using this methodology, Pardee found a correlation coefficient for his regression line of .89, significantly positive, and a coefficient of determination of .79.[24] He concluded that "differences in industrial composition 'explained' about 80% of the variance of actual average earnings for manufacturing production workers across the country. Generally we can predict that an area will have high or low wages depending upon the high or low wage character of its dominant industries."[25]

In an earlier survey, Hanna had used similar methodology in comparing wage levels among the states. He concluded that as of 1949 "industrial composition, *together with the forces correlated with it,* appear to explain up to 70 per cent of the reported interstate earning differentials"[26] (emphasis added).

The difficulty with Pardee's and Hanna's type of analysis is that the factors correlated with industrial composition may provide the real explanation for a high coefficient of determination. Different industries have different labor-force skill requirements. It is conceivable, therefore, that interarea wage differentials should be attributed to differences in the level of skill among areas.

In fact, Hanna has also calculated a coefficient of determination of .87 by correlating average earnings in each state with "rate constant" occupational earnings for the same state.[27] This is the average earning rate which would prevail in a state if every employee in that state earned the national average wage rate for his occupation.

Although Hanna is aware of the problems involved in using correlation techniques, he seems to conclude in this study that occupational differences are primarily responsible for interstate differences in earning rates. Denison has taken strong exception to this conclusion.[28] He reorganizes Hanna's own data and concludes that less than 30 per cent of the interarea wage differentials can be ascribed to occupational differences and that the remainder is explained by other factors. However, Denison goes on to point out that available data are insufficient to provide a statistically reliable conclusion with multiple correlation analysis.

The classical and industrial-composition explanations of interarea wage differentials are closely linked through the industrial-location process. As a result, it is difficult to devise statistical techniques which allocate responsibility between the two theories. This close connection is well illustrated in Figure 1.

Most cities in Figure 1 are concentrated in the Northeast or Southwest Quadrants. In other words, high-wage industries are in locations with positive "area effects," and low-wage industries are located in areas with negative "area effects."* A logical explanation is

---

* Pardee explains the "industry effect" and the "area effect" in Figure 1 as follows:

"As an example, consider Providence, Rhode Island. In June 1960, the average hourly earnings of production workers in manufacturing in Providence was $1.86. This was 43¢ below the United States average hourly earnings of $2.29 taken for all areas and industries. Close to half of the manufacturing workers in Providence were in the textile and jewelry industries; both low wage. For June 1960 the national average hourly earnings in the Textile Mill Products Industry was $1.63; in the Jewelry, Silverware, and Plated Wire Industry, $1.96. By taking all industries operating in Providence and assuming that each firm paid the national average hourly earnings for its industry, I

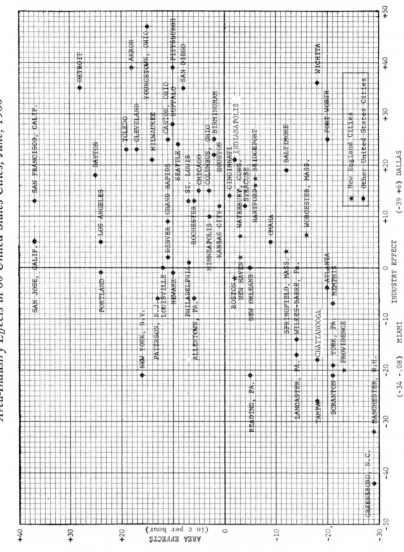

FIGURE 1

Area-Industry Effects in 60 United States Cities, June, 1960

SOURCE: Scott E. Pardee, "A Study of Inter-City Wage Differentials" (unpublished Ph.D. dissertation, Department of Economics and Social Science, Massachusetts Institute of Technology, 1962), Table V, 1, pp. 97–98.

that high-wage areas are favorably situated with respect to such factors as markets, supplies of raw materials, industrial fuels, and electrical energy. Industries such as steel, chemicals, petroleum, automobiles, primary metals, and heavy machinery have specific locational requirements, and they generally locate in these favorably situated areas. Such basic industries attract satellite industries, and there is rapid industrial growth.

The resulting wage level in almost all favorably located labor markets is high for three reasons:

1. Firms in heavy industry, wherever they are located, tend to pay above national average wages for particular skills. They can afford to pay high wages because labor costs comprise a small fraction of total costs and there is an inelastic demand for their output. In addition, unions are usually very effective in organizing and negotiating in heavy industry.

2. The high level of wages in heavy industry sometimes spills over into the wage structures of related industries operating in the same area. Although large differentials in wage rates can and do exist among firms hiring labor in the same area, some firms cannot maintain the morale of their labor force if other nearby firms in related industries are paying much higher wages.

3. As a result of rapid economic growth in favorably located areas, the local demand for labor exceeds the local supply. Employers bid up the price of labor, and the final result is a wage level which attracts employees from the surrounding region.

To the extent that wage levels in favorably located metropolitan areas are raised by the competitive actions of a large number of growing firms, the resulting high wage structure is explained by the classical theory of interarea wage differentials. To the extent, however, that the wage levels in high-wage cities are "artificially high" as a result of strong unions and the market power of the dominant employers,

computed an industry weighted average hourly earning rate for that city. This rate was $2.09, 20¢ below the United States average for all areas and industries. The 20¢ is called the 'industry effect.' The difference of 23¢ between the industry weighted average hourly earnings, $2.09, and the actual average hourly earnings, $1.86, I called the 'area effect.' Thus, Providence had actual average hourly earnings 43¢ below the national average, 20¢ of which was directly due to the low wage character of the industries located there, and 23¢ due to other forces affecting wage levels in the area."[29]

the wage structure is explained by the "industrial composition" theory of interarea wage differentials.

In any event, the resulting high wage level hurts the competitive position of the labor-intensive industries originally located in the area. It also discourages additional manufacturing firms in low-wage labor-intensive industries from moving to the area. Thus, high-wage industries tend to be grouped together in high-wage areas. Labor-intensive industries are forced to remain in New England,* the South, and other low-wage areas.

As a result, it is very difficult to use correlation analysis to determine the extent to which industrial composition explains interarea wage differentials. Labor-intensive industries are attracted to low-wage areas; capital-intensive industries cluster in favorably located metropolitan areas. Why are high wage levels maintained in these favorably located areas? The answer obviously varies from labor market to labor market. Sometimes the demand for labor exceeds the supply, and wages are bid up. In other cases a concentration of heavy industry determines that wage levels will be high. In some cases both forces are of equal importance. The point is, however, that the clustering of capital-intensive industries in high-wage areas is entirely compatible with both the classical and industrial-composition theories.

Correlating industrial composition with average industrial wage rates leaves other questions unanswered. For example, the unusually high level of wage rates in labor markets such as San Francisco and Detroit can only partially be explained by industrial composition (see Figure 1). Should the remainder be attributed to the classical theory or to the spill-over from industrial composition? The situation is probably different in each of these major labor markets. Spill-over is probably important in Detroit; the classical theory may provide the best explanation in San Francisco.

----

* Figure 1 shows that six of the nine metropolitan areas in New England have a small *positive* "industry effect." However, the metropolitan areas in New England with the lowest wage rates (New Bedford, Fall River, Lawrence-Haverhill, Lowell, and Brockton) are not shown in Figure 1. In these labor markets, the available employment data were not sufficiently detailed to permit Pardee to separate the "area effect" from the "industry effect." Also most high-wage industries in New England have unusually high skill requirements.

Finally, wages in most metropolitan areas are higher than the average manufacturing wage rate in the nation, which includes wages in industries such as lumber, food, textiles, and apparel, which are often located in small towns.

Chapter V

UNEMPLOYMENT, MIGRATION, AND MANUFACTURING WAGE RATES IN NEW ENGLAND

According to the modified classical explanation of interarea wage differentials, unemployment and low wage rates do not induce sufficient out-migration to diminish the supply of labor in most depressed areas. Although net out-migration may be substantial, it is generally much less than the natural population increase. Consequently, the supply of labor in depressed areas increases from year to year. At the same time the demand for labor is weaker in poorly endowed areas than in other parts of the country. The net result is that wage rates remain well below national average levels.

The history of unemployment, migration, and manufacturing wage rates in New England provides support for this modified version of the classical supply-demand theory. As shown in Chapter IV, however, the industrial-composition theory may provide the best single explanation for the manufacturing wage levels which exist in metropolitan areas such as Detroit, Pittsburgh, and Buffalo. Thus, both the classical and the industrial-composition theories help explain wage differentials among metropolitan areas and regions in the United States.

New England's Population and Migration History

New England has had relatively low manufacturing wage rates for a long time, particularly in the three northern states. Nevertheless, Table 10 shows that the population of New England and each of its constitutent states has increased almost continuously for the last ninety years. This has occurred despite the decline of farming in the

59

TABLE 10

*Decennial Rates of Increase in Population, New England and the United States,
1870–1960*

Percentage changes

Area	1870–80	1880–90	1890–00	1900–10	1910–20	1920–30	1930–40	1940–50	1950–60
Maine	3.5	1.9	5.0	6.9	3.5	3.8	6.2	7.9	6.1
New Hampshire	9.0	8.5	9.3	4.6	2.9	5.0	5.6	8.5	13.8
Vermont	0.5	—	3.4	3.6	–1.0	2.0	–0.1	5.2	3.2
Massachusetts	22.4	25.6	25.3	20.0	14.4	10.3	1.6	8.7	9.8
Rhode Island	27.2	24.9	24.0	26.6	11.4	13.7	3.8	11.0	8.5
Connecticut	15.9	19.8	21.7	22.7	23.9	16.4	6.4	17.4	26.3
Northern N.E. (Me., N.H., Vt.)	4.1	3.1	5.8	5.5	2.3	3.8	4.7	7.5	7.7
Southern N.E. (Mass., R.I., Conn.)	21.3	24.2	24.4	21.3	16.2	12.1	3.0	11.1	14.1
NEW ENGLAND	15.0	17.2	19.0	17.2	12.9	10.3	3.3	10.4	12.8
UNITED STATES	30.1	25.5	20.7	21.0	15.0	16.2	7.3	14.5	18.5

SOURCE: U.S. Bureau of the Census, *U.S. Census of Population: 1960.* Vol. I. *Characteristics of the Population.* Part A. *Number of Inhabitants* (Washington, D.C.: U.S. Government Printing Office, 1961), Tables 9 and 10.

nineteenth century and the loss of much of the textile industry to the South in the twentieth century.

The region's population growth rate has been slow. In most decades since 1870 it has been between one-half and three-quarters of the national rate. The northern New England states (where wage rates have been very low) have had very little growth; in two decades Vermont had a slight population decrease. Considering the decline of farming and the textile industry, these data might be interpreted to mean that migration from New England has been very substantial but that the natural population increase has been even larger, and that the net result has been a continuing population increase with below national average growth rates.

This would be an accurate interpretation for the three northern New England states. In these states, the natural population increase has consistently overwhelmed substantial population losses resulting from net out-migration. In the three southern New England states and in the region as a whole, however, other factors have played more important roles.

As shown in Table 11, in most decades since 1870 there has been net *in*-migration to the New England region. Despite this trend, the region's population growth rate has always lagged behind that of the nation. Low fertility rates have had a very significant influence. Until recent decades, the region's average fertility rate has been between 70 and 90 per cent of the national average rate. These low fertility rates, in turn, can be explained by the small percentage of persons living in rural locations in the region. In New England, as in the nation, rural families have had more children than urban families. The region's population growth has also been curtailed by higher than national average mortality rates. Because of foreign *in*-migration and native-born *out*-migration, New England's population has always included a high percentage of foreign-born persons, who have a slightly lower life expectancy than native-born persons.

FOREIGN IN-MIGRATION

Table 11 shows that New England has always attracted migrants from foreign countries. Unskilled immigrants have been employed by the textile, apparel, shoe, jewelry, and furniture industries. Although these are "low wage" industries in the United States, wages here are much higher than in any foreign country.

TABLE 11

Net Intercensal Migration, New England,
1870–1960

Area	1870–80	1880–90	1890–00	1900–10	1910–20
NEW ENGLAND					
Total Net Migration	+141,100	+402,600	+493,700	+496,200	+297,600
Native white	− 67,200	− 32,700	+ 21,600	− 80,400	− 53,000
Foreign-born white	+203,800	+428,700	+457,700	+568,800	+338,600
Negro	+ 4,600	+ 6,700	+ 14,500	+ 7,900	+ 12,000

Area	1920–30	1930–40	1940–50	1950–60[a]	CENSUS BUREAU 1940–50	1950–60
NEW ENGLAND						
Total Net Migration	+ 27,500	− 43,400	− 6,000	− 29,800	+101,000	+ 23,000
Native white	−190,200	− 23,100	−105,000	−138,500		
Foreign-born white	+210,600	− 25,600	+ 74,000	+ 59,400		
Negro	+ 7,400	+ 5,100	+ 25,000	+ 49,200		

[a] Estimates, based on methods described by Lee *et al.*

SOURCES: 1870–1950 series: Everett S. Lee *et al., Population Redistribution and Economic Growth: United States, 1870–1950.* Vol. I. *Methodological Considerations and Reference Tables* (Philadelphia: The American Philosophical Society, 1957), Reference Table P-1, pp. 107–231.

1940–1960 series: U.S. Bureau of the Census, *Current Population Reports,* Series P-25, No. 227, "Preliminary Estimates of the Components of Population Change, by States: 1950 to 1960" (Washington, D.C.: U.S. Government Printing Office, 1961).

The big surge in immigration occurred in the period 1890 to 1910, when New England gained over a million foreign-born persons. Federal legislation has since curtailed immigration, but a substantial net in-migration of foreign-born persons has continued. It is probable that many of the recent immigrants have wished to join earlier immigrants who speak the same language, have the same religion, and enjoy the same type of social life. In most recent decades the foreign-born in-migration has about equaled the out-migration of native-born persons.

As a result of the in-migration of the foreign-born and the out-migration of the native-born, a very substantial part of the population in New England is foreign-born or has foreign-born parents. Table 12 shows that except for New York, no part of the country has as large a proportion of foreign stock in its population as does southern New England.

THE OUT-MIGRATION OF THE NATIVE-BORN

Native-born persons between twenty and forty years of age have been leaving New England in significant numbers ever since 1870. Young adults are generally mobile, and most native-born persons in New England have had a good schooling, speak good English, have learned basic skills, and are readily accepted in all parts of the country. They have the option of accepting higher-paying jobs in other regions.

The vast majority of them have chosen to remain in the region, however. During most decades since 1870, the net migration of native-born white persons between the ages of twenty and forty years in New England has generally amounted to less than 5 per cent of the total population of this group. The out-migration for native-born persons of all ages has usually not exceeded 2 per cent. This low percentage compares with a natural population increase for all native-born persons which has always been 10 per cent or more and which in most decades has exceeded 15 per cent.

INTRAREGIONAL MIGRATION

Compared with the sluggish migration between New England and other regions, the movement of population between states and within states in the region has been brisk in most decades since 1870. The

TABLE 12

States with Greatest Relative Concentration of White Foreign-Born and White Children of Foreign-Born, 1920, 1950, and 1960

	1920			1950			1960	
Rank	State	Percentage of Total White Population	Rank	State	Percentage of Total White Population	Rank	State	Percentage of Total White Population
1	Rhode Island	70.8	1	Rhode Island	49.9	1	New York	41.2
2	Massachusetts	67.6	2	Connecticut	49.5	2	Massachusetts	40.5
3	North Dakota	67.5	3	Massachusetts	49.5	3	Connecticut	40.2
4	Connecticut	66.9	4	New York	49.2	4	Rhode Island	40.1
5	Minnesota	65.1	5	New Jersey	44.8	5	New Jersey	37.7
6	New York	63.9	6	North Dakota	39.6	6	North Dakota	30.5
7	New Jersey	60.1	7	New Hampshire	36.1	7	New Hampshire	29.2
8	Wisconsin	59.7	8	Minnesota	34.7	8	Illinois	26.9
9	Michigan	53.6	9	Illinois	33.4	9	Michigan	26.6
10	Illinois	51.3	10	Michigan	33.3	10	Minnesota	25.8
12	New Hampshire	49.0	15	Maine	27.1	15	Maine	23.3
24	Maine	35.3	18	Vermont	25.6	18	Vermont	22.0
25	Vermont	35.1		UNITED STATES[a]	25.0		UNITED STATES[a]	20.8
	UNITED STATES[a]	38.4						

[a] United States excluding Alaska and Hawaii.

SOURCES: U.S. Bureau of the Census, *Fourteenth Census of the United States: 1920. Vol. III. Population* (Washington, D.C.: U.S. Government Printing Office, 1922), Table 7, p. 19.

———, *U.S. Census of Population: 1950. Vol. IV*, Part 3. Chapter A (Washington, D.C.: U.S. Government Printing Office, 1954), pp. 17, 20–44.

———, *U.S. Census of Population: 1960. General Social and Economic Characteristics, United States Summary* (Series PC [1]) (Washington, D.C.: U.S. Government Printing Office, 1962), Table 108.

movement of population has been continuous from stagnant low-wage areas to faster-growing higher-wage areas *within* the region. For example, from 1950 to 1960, the out-migration of native-born whites between the ages of twenty and forty from New England as a whole amounted to only 2.9 per cent of the 1960 population of that age group. During the same decade, there was a 10.7 per cent out-migration from Maine and 16.3 per cent from Vermont. Of the six states, only Connecticut has consistently had a net in-migration of native-born whites in recent decades. From 1950 to 1960 Connecticut had a 12.5 per cent net in-migration of native-born whites between the ages of twenty and forty. In the same decade, many small towns in northern New England lost most of their young people, while the young native-born population of certain suburbs in Greater Boston and Greater Hartford trebled.

The varying population patterns shown on Figure 2 can be explained by differing wage rates and job opportunities in various parts of the region. In New England, as in the United States, better job opportunities exist in urban areas. Furthermore, wages in Connecticut tend to be the highest in New England, followed by those in Massachusetts.

New England continues to supply jobs for the majority of the children born in the region. However, it is usually quite difficult for persons in northern New England to find acceptable employment nearby. Although cities such as Burlington, Vermont, and Portland, Maine, offer some opportunity, many young people migrate to southern New England.

CONCLUSIONS

Thus New England's migration history generally supports the modified classical theory of interarea and interregional wage differentials. Migrants have moved from low-wage countries outside the United States to New England and from New England to higher-wage regions within the United States. Furthermore, the movement of population within the region has been from relatively low-wage areas to higher-wage areas. The migration has been from rural to urban areas, from the three northern New England states to Massachusetts and Connecticut, and from Massachusetts and Rhode Island to Connecticut. Nevertheless, as shown in Chapter III and in Appendix A, large

FIGURE 2-A
Population Increases, New England, 1950–1960

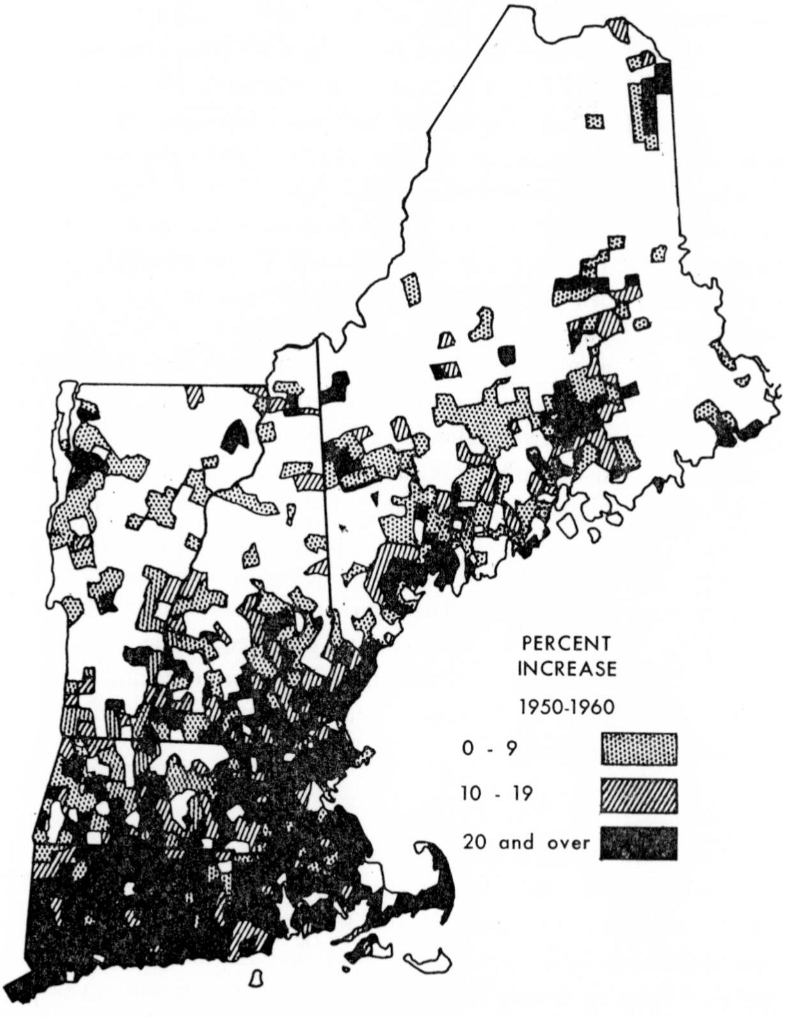

SOURCE: "The Roving Population," *New England Business Review: Federal Reserve Bank of Boston,* October, 1960, p. 7.

FIGURE 2-B
Population Decreases, New England, 1950–1960

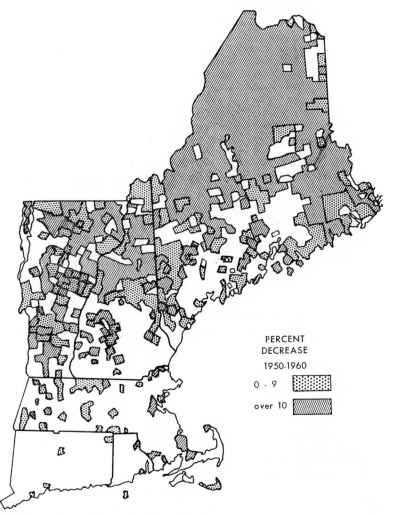

PERCENT
DECREASE
1950-1960

0 - 9

over 10

SOURCE: "The Roving Population," *New England Business Review: Federal Reserve Bank of Boston,* October, 1960, p. 7.

wage differentials continue to exist among New England's labor markets and between the region's labor markets and those in other regions.

The Impact of Unemployment on Manufacturing Wage Rates in New England—1947–1960

In 1949, 26 per cent of the labor force was unemployed in Lawrence, Massachusetts, and 18 per cent in New Bedford, Massachusetts. Table 13 provides metropolitan area unemployment data for the period from 1948 (when labor-market unemployment data were first published in this form) through 1960. During this period five New England metropolitan areas had a large surplus of labor most of the time. Two other areas had a substantial surplus of labor much of the time. Table 14 shows that every New England state had a total unemployment rate which was well above the national average in 1950. No other region in the country had such serious unemployment during this prosperous period.

New England's textile industry was largely responsible for this catastrophe. Starting in 1949, the region's textile employment declined rapidly. Substantial increases in productivity, a slow growth in the demand for textile products, and stiff competition from low-cost southern mills all contributed to the slump.[1]

Subsequently, the transportation equipment industry in Connecticut and the electronics industry in Massachusetts replaced this loss. As a result, by 1960 four of the six New England states had unemployment rates slightly *below* the national average. Furthermore, since 1960 the unemployment rates in all the New England states have moved down to or below the national average. Nevertheless, the postwar record up until 1960 was one of chronic labor surplus.[2]

Table 13 provides substantial evidence supporting the classical theory of interarea wage differentials. It lists New England cities according to their average level of unemployment in the period between 1948 and 1960. The labor markets at the top of the list had a continuous labor shortage during this period. Those at the bottom of the list had chronic unemployment. Manufacturing wages declined relative to the United States average in every labor market where the unemployment rate was higher than 6 per cent for more than one-third of the time between 1948 and 1960. The metropolitan areas with

TABLE 13

Gross Average Hourly Earnings of Production Workers in Manufacturing
as a Percentage of the United States Average, and Changes
in Total Manufacturing Employment, Selected
New England Labor Markets,
1951 and 1961

New England Labor Market Area	Status of Labor Market (Nov. 1948 to Nov. 1960)	Annual Average of Hourly Earnings (U.S. = 100)		Percentage Change in	
		1951	1961	Earnings 1951	Employ-ment to 1961
Hartford, Conn.	Tight: 77% of time less than 3% unemployed	107.7	106.9	+47.6	+17.5
Stamford, Conn.	Tight: 64% of time less than 3% unemployed	107.7	107.8	+48.8	+14.4
New Haven, Conn.	Tight: 62% of time less than 3% unemployed	94.2	101.3	+59.9	− 2.9
Boston, Mass.	Balanced: 12% of time less than 3% unem-ployed; 8% of time 6% or more unem-ployed	98.1	100.9	+52.9	− 1.9
New Britain, Conn.	Usually balanced: 28% of time 6% or more unemployed; 46% of time less than 3% un-employed	100.0	102.6	+52.6	−23.3
Bridgeport, Conn.	Usually balanced: 29% of time 6% or more unemployed; 41% of time less than 3% un-employed	103.8	106.0	+51.9	− 2.4

TABLE 13 (continued)

New England Labor Market Area	Status of Labor Market (Nov. 1948 to Nov. 1960)	Annual Average of Hourly Earnings (U.S. = 100)		Percentage Change in	
		1951	1961	Earnings 1951 to 1961	Employment 1951 to 1961
Waterbury, Conn.	Usually balanced: 27% of time 6% or more unemployed; 36% of time less than 3% unemployed	100.0	103.4	+53.8	−17.6
Portland, Me.	Surplus labor: 24% of time 6% or more unemployed; 7% of time less than 3% unemployed	84.0	87.9	+55.7	0.0
Worcester, Mass.	Surplus labor: 26% of time 6% or more unemployed; 7% of time less than 3% unemployed	105.8	97.8	+37.6	−18.0
Manchester, N.H.	Surplus labor: 21% of time 6% or more unemployed; 1% of time less than 3% unemployed	66.5	75.0	+28.9	−17.1
Springfield-Holyoke, Mass.	Surplus labor: 34% of time 6% or more unemployed	100.0	97.0	+44.2	− 7.3
Brockton, Mass.	Surplus labor: 43% of time 6% or more unemployed	n.a.	81.0	n.a.	n.a.

TABLE 13 (continued)

New England Labor Market Area	Status of Labor Market (Nov. 1948 to Nov. 1960)	Annual Average of Hourly Earnings (U.S. = 100)		Percentage Change in	
		1951	1961	Earnings 1951 to 1961	Employment 1951 to 1961
New Bedford, Mass.	Very substantial surplus labor: 63% of time 6% or more unemployed	86.5	76.7	+31.9	−26.0
Fall River, Mass.	Very substantial surplus labor: 71% of time 6% or more unemployed	80.1	74.1	+37.6	−16.2
Providence, R.I.	Very substantial surplus labor: 99% of time 6% or more unemployed	89.1	82.3	+37.4	−21.8
Lowell, Mass.	Very substantial surplus labor: 100% of time 6% or more unemployed	n.a.	84.9	n.a.	n.a.
Lawrence-Haverhill, Mass.	Very substantial surplus labor: 100% of time 6% or more unemployed	n.a.	86.6	n.a.	n.a.

SOURCES: U.S. Bureau of Employment Security, *The Labor Market and Employment Security, 1948–1960.*
U.S. Bureau of Labor Statistics, *Employment and Earnings, Annual Supplement Issue,* Vol. VIII, No. 12 (June, 1962).
———, *Employment and Earnings Statistics for the United States: 1909–1960* (Bulletin No. 1312) (Washington, D.C.: U.S. Government Printing Office, 1961).
Unpublished data furnished by U.S. Bureau of Labor Statistics, New England Regional Office, Boston, Mass., and co-operating State Departments of Labor and Industries and State Divisions of Employment Security.

TABLE 14

Unemployment as a Percentage of Civilian Labor Force,
New England and the United States,
1950 and 1960

	Total		Male		Female	
	1950	*1960*	*1950*	*1960*	*1950*	*1960*
Maine	8.8	6.5	9.5	6.3	6.9	6.8
New Hampshire	6.6	4.3	7.2	3.9	5.2	4.8
Vermont	5.5	4.5	5.7	4.5	4.7	4.5
Massachusetts	5.8	4.2	6.4	4.3	4.4	4.0
Rhode Island	7.2	5.3	8.1	4.7	5.4	6.4
Connecticut	5.4	4.6	5.6	3.9	4.9	5.8
NEW ENGLAND	6.1	4.6	6.7	4.4	4.8	4.9
UNITED STATES	4.8	5.1	5.2	5.0	4.6	5.4

SOURCES: U.S. Bureau of the Census, *U.S. Census of Population: 1960. Detailed Characteristics.* Connecticut, Maine, Massachusetts, New Hampshire, Rhode Island, and Vermont (separate publication for each state) (Washington, D.C.: U.S. Government Printing Office, 1962), Table 115.
————, *U.S. Census of Population: 1950.* Vol. II. *Characteristics of the Population.* Part 1. *United States Summary* (Washington, D.C.: U.S. Government Printing Office, 1953), Tables 72 and 73.

tight labor markets improved their wage standings or remained well above the national average.

The data in Table 15 provide additional and more or less conclusive evidence of the dominant importance of the classical theory in New England. During the post–World War II period, manufacturing wage rates in the region did not increase as fast as those in the nation. As a result, the average level of manufacturing wages declined from 95.5 per cent of the national average in 1947 to 93.0 per cent in 1958. Of the national increase in manufacturing wages of 36.2 per cent in this period, only 2.2 per cent can be attributed to the rapid growth of industries with above national average wage rates. In New England, on the other hand, 3.1 per cent is explained by an improved industrial structure. Nevertheless, New England manufacturing wage rates declined relative to those in the nation during this period. Thus, in New England the negative impact of unemployment and the lack of migration (the classical theory) overwhelmed the positive impact of a relatively fast growth in high-wage industries (the industrial-composition theory) to bring about a declining relative regional manufacturing wage level.

TABLE 15

Wage Changes Resulting from Shifts in Industrial Structure, New England and the United States, 1947, 1954, and 1958

1947–1954

	Average Hourly Wage 1947 (1947 dollars)	Average Hourly Wage 1954 (1947 dollars)	Average Hourly Wage in 1954 Using 1947 Employment Weights[a] (1947 dollars)	Percentage Increase 1947–1954		Percentage Difference Caused by Structural Change
				Actual	Without Structural Change	
NEW ENGLAND	$1.306	$1.571	$1.556	20.3	19.1	1.2
UNITED STATES	1.368	1.687	1.669	23.3	22.0	1.3

1954–1958

	Average Hourly Wage 1954 (1947 dollars)	Average Hourly Wage 1958 (1947 dollars)	Average Hourly Wage in 1958 Using 1954 Employment Weights[a] (1947 dollars)	Percentage Increase 1954–1958		Percentage Difference Caused by Structural Change
				Actual	Without Structural Change	
NEW ENGLAND	$1.571	$1.733	$1.723	10.3	9.7	0.6
UNITED STATES	1.687	1.863	1.860	10.4	10.3	0.1

See footnotes at end of table.

TABLE 15 (continued)

	Average Hourly Wage 1947 (1947 dollars)	Average Hourly Wage 1958 (1947 dollars)	Average Hourly Wage in 1958 Using 1947 Employment Weights[a] (1947 dollars)	Percentage Increase 1947–1958		Percentage Difference Caused by Structural Change
				Actual	Without Structural Change	
NEW ENGLAND	$1.306	$1.733	$1.693	32.7	29.6	3.1
UNITED STATES	1.368	1.863	1.833	36.2	34.0	2.2

[a] This column is computed by weighting the most recent wage level in each four-digit industry (such as 1954) with the earlier census year's employment weight (such as 1947).

NOTE: The undeflated average wages for New England and the United States in 1947, 1954, and 1958, on which this table is based, were computed by the same method as those in Table 3, p. 28ff. They differ slightly, however, because they are based on a more complete coverage of four-digit industries.

SOURCES: U.S. Bureau of the Census, *Census of Manufactures: 1947* (Washington, D.C.: U.S. Government Printing Office, 1949–1950).

―――, *U.S. Census of Manufactures: 1954* (Washington, D.C.: U.S. Government Printing Office, 1957).

―――, *U.S. Census of Manufactures: 1958* (Preliminary Reports Series MC[P]) (Washington, D.C.: U.S. Government Printing Office, 1959–1960).

―――, *U.S. Census of Manufactures: 1958* (Washington, D.C.: U.S. Government Printing Office, 1961).

U.S. Bureau of Labor Statistics, *Prices: A Chartbook 1953–62* (Bulletin No. 1351) (Washington, D.C.: U.S. Government Printing Office, December, 1962), Table A, p. 118.

Conclusions

New England's population has grown and continues to grow at a much slower rate than the population in the United States. This slow growth is attributable to unique demographic characteristics and to a limited amount of out-migration of young native-born adults.

In general, however, intraregional migration has been much more important than interregional migration. A substantial number of people continue to move from northern New England to southern New England, from rural to metropolitan areas, and from depressed to prosperous areas. Thus, the region's labor force has responded to the higher income opportunities available in its better-located areas. However, the response has not been sufficient to eliminate wage differentials among labor markets within the region.

The available evidence strongly suggests that the modified classical theory best explains wage movements in New England. As mentioned in Chapter IV, however, the industrial-composition theory may be more useful in explaining the existence of relatively high wage levels in labor markets such as Pittsburgh, Detroit, and Buffalo. Thus, the difference between low average manufacturing wage rates in New England and high average manufacturing wages in the Midwest and elsewhere may be best explained by using both wage theories.

Chapter VI

MANUFACTURING SPECIALIZATION IN NEW ENGLAND

CHAPTER II provided a detailed description of New England's geographical handicaps. The region has high fuel and power costs and lacks access to raw materials and national markets. As a result of these disadvantages, the region cannot attract most types of manufacturing requiring substantial amounts of fuel and energy for processing materials which would ultimately be shipped to national markets.

This chapter will show how manufacturing firms in New England have gradually adapted to the region's harsh economic climate. Except in the textile industry, very few firms have relocated. However, established firms have changed their product lines, and new firms have chosen products which can be manufactured profitably in the region.

Unless they serve a local market, New England manufacturers usually produce either specialty items or technical products. This type of manufacturing typically requires that a large number of man-hours be devoted to a small volume of raw materials to create a high-value product. Thus, the region's producers avoid mass-production goods and concentrate on items that must be manufactured with a labor-intensive technology using semiskilled and skilled labor. They do this because the cost of trained labor is the only major cost that is lower in New England than in most other regions.

Firms in every important New England industry manufacture specialties. Nonintegrated paper companies sell a great variety of industrial and technical papers.[1] The furniture industry creates high-quality merchandise or items such as doll furniture.[2] The textile industry produces unique products for the New York City market.[3] A manufacturer of drop forgings sells specialty hand tools.[4] Producers of electronic parts, instruments, and machinery design, engineer, and manufacture tailor-made equipment for industry and the Department of Defense.[5]

Specialty items are usually labor-intensive products. However, some items which cannot be classified as "specialties" are also labor-intensive. Aircraft engines, one of Connecticut's most important products, are an excellent example. The computers manufactured in metropolitan Boston are another. Although computers are a symbol of modern automated technology, they must be manufactured with labor-intensive techniques. The 1963 Census of Manufactures shows that 66 per cent of value added in the manufacture of computers is accounted for by wage and salary payments. This percentage is one of the highest for four-digit industries.

Measuring Labor Intensity

The remainder of this chapter provides statistical evidence that the trend toward labor-intensive manufacturing has progressed rather rapidly in New England in the post–World War II period. This is true whether the use of labor is measured against the use of electrical energy, the use of fuel, or the use of capital equipment.

THE RATIO OF ELECTRICAL ENERGY USE TO THE NUMBER OF MANUFACTURING EMPLOYEES

Table 16 shows that manufacturing firms located in New England do not use large amounts of electrical energy. In 1947, electrical energy consumption per manufacturing employee in the United States was 168 per cent of the consumption in New England. By 1958, this percentage had increased to 240 per cent. In 1962, electrical energy consumption per employee remained at about the 1958 level.

The data clearly show that New England manufacturing firms avoid processes which require substantial use of electricity. The data also suggest that the region's manufacturing employees work with the assistance of less power-driven equipment than do employees in the nation.

THE RATIO OF FUEL USE TO THE NUMBER OF MANUFACTURING EMPLOYEES

The historical record of fuel use in New England and the United States is incomplete. However, Table 17 shows that fuel consumption per employee in United States manufacturing in 1962 was 236 per

TABLE 16

Electric Power Consumption per Manufacturing Employee,
New England and the United States,
1947, 1954, 1958, and 1962

Area	Kilowatt-hours Consumed (millions)	Manufacturing Employment[a]	Kilowatt-hours per Employee	Comparison of United States with New England (N.E. = 100)
1947				
New England	8,681	1,475,162	5,884.8	
United States	140,947	14,293,963	9,850.6	168
1954				
New England	10,519	1,431,298	7,349.3	
United States	247,666	15,645,491	15,829.9	215
1958				
New England	11,774	1,359,919	8,657.9	
United States	319,262	15,394,010	20,739.4	240
1962				
New England	14,792	1,434,693	10,310.2	
United States	387,110	16,135,501	23,991.2	233

[a] Employment in operating manufacturing establishments, excluding central administrative offices and auxiliary units. United States excluding Alaska and Hawaii.

SOURCES: U.S. Bureau of the Census, *Census of Manufactures: 1947.* Vol. I. *Summary Statistics* (Washington, D.C.: U.S. Government Printing Office, 1950), Table 3, p. 221.

———, *U.S. Census of Manufactures: 1958.* Vol. I. *Summary Statistics* (Washington, D.C.: U.S. Government Printing Office, 1961), Table 4, p. 6–22 and Table 6, p. 1–44.

———, *Annual Survey of Manufactures: 1962* (Washington, D.C.: U.S. Government Printing Office, 1964), Table 2, pp. 16–17; Chapter III, Geographic Statistics, pp. 54–57, 244–263.

———, *Census of Manufactures: 1963. Fuels and Electric Energy Consumed by Manufacturing Industries: 1962* (Preliminary Report MC63[PI-2) (Washington, D.C.: U.S. Government Printing Office, January 8, 1964), Table 5, p. 13.

TABLE 17

Fuel Consumption per Manufacturing Employee,
New England and the United States,
1962

	New England	United States
Total Manufacturing Employment[a]	1,434,693	16,162,677
Coal Consumed (1,000 tons)	2,093	89,133
Average Btu's per ton[b] (000)	26,722	24,050
Average Btu's per employee	38,983,355	132,629,554
Oil Consumed (1,000 barrels)	33,988	191,836
Average Btu's per barrel[b]	6,284,460	6,332,088
Average Btu's per employee	148,879,395	75,156,017
Gas Consumed (million cubic feet)	28,260	4,396,417
Average Btu's per cubic foot[b]	1,004	1,034
Average Btu's per employee	19,776,384	281,258,802
Total Btu's per employee	207,639,134	489,044,373
Comparison of United States with New England (N.E. = 100)	100	236

[a] Employment in operating manufacturing establishments, excluding central administrative offices and auxiliary units. United States including Alaska and Hawaii.

[b] Based on average number of Btu's per unit of each of three types of fuel used for electric generation as found by analysis of the total electric utility industry, shown in the *Statistical Yearbook of the Electric Utility Industry for 1963.*

SOURCES: U.S. Bureau of the Census, *Annual Survey of Manufactures: 1962* (Washington, D.C.: U.S. Government Printing Office, 1964), Table 2, p. 16; Chapter III, Geographic Statistics, pp. 54–57.

Edison Electric Institute, *Statistical Yearbook of the Electric Utility Industry for 1963* (New York: Edison Electric Institute, September, 1964), Table 42S, p. 44.

U.S. Bureau of the Census, *Census of Manufactures: 1963. Fuels and Electric Energy Consumed by Manufacturing Industries: 1962* (Preliminary Report MC63[P]–2) (Washington, D.C.: U.S. Government Printing Office, January 8, 1964), Table 5, p. 13.

cent of the consumption rate in New England. This compares with 229 per cent in 1958. It is evident that New England manufacturers avoid products which must be processed with large quantities of industrial fuel as would be typically required in capital-intensive industries which involve the processing of large volumes of raw materials.

LABOR INTENSITY AS MEASURED BY PERLOFF ET AL.

Harvey S. Perloff and his collaborators have recently produced estimates of the capital-labor ratios used in each manufacturing industry in the United States.[6] They calculated the "capital" in each industry in two ways. One estimate of the value of "capital" was based on unpublished statistics produced by Daniel Creamer for each industry in the United States in 1948. The other estimate was made by subtracting the compensation of employees in each industry from national income by industrial origin in 1948. The results are equal to profits before taxes plus net interest paid. The latter estimate provides a measure of return to capital, rather than a direct measure of capital.

Perloff *et al.* have divided both measures of capital by the number of full-time employees in each industry to obtain two different indices of capital intensity. Both measures indicate that eight industries have below average capital intensity. Both indices show that five other industries are capital-intensive. The results are conflicting for the remaining four industries. Perloff *et al.* have categorized each industry as follows:

LABOR-INTENSIVE (*by both measures*)	CAPITAL-INTENSIVE (*by both measures*)
(1) Lumber and furniture products	(1) Tobacco
(2) Apparel and related products	(2) Paper
(3) Textile-mill products	(3) Chemicals
(4) Printing	(4) Petroleum and coal
(5) Leather and related products	(5) Motor vehicles
(6) Machinery (except electrical)	
(7) Electrical machinery	(*by one measure*)
(8) Transportation equipment	(6) Food
(except motor vehicles)	(7) Metals, metal products, and miscellaneous
	(8) Stone, clay, and glass
	(9) Rubber

Perloff *et al.*'s broad category "metals, metal products, and miscellaneous" includes certain industries which are clearly not capital-intensive. For example, the miscellaneous category includes manufacture of jewelry, silverware, and notions. In the calculations

FIGURE 3

Manufacturing Employment in High Capital–Labor Ratio Industries, 1950

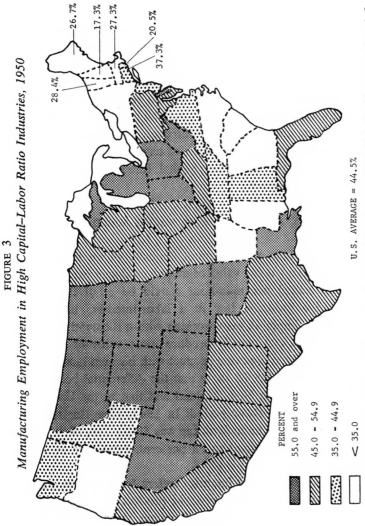

PERCENT

55.0 and over

45.0 – 54.9

35.0 – 44.9

< 35.0

U. S. AVERAGE = 44.5%

26.7%

17.3%

27.3%

20.5%

28.4%

37.3%

SOURCE: U.S. Bureau of the Census, *U.S. Census of Population: 1950. Vol. II. Characteristics of the Population* (Washington, D.C.: U.S. Government Printing Office, 1952), Table 79.

for Figure 3, the Perloff *et al.* data have been adjusted to classify instrument and miscellaneous manufacturing as labor-intensive.

Figure 3 clearly shows that as of 1950 the New England and southeastern states specialized in labor-intensive manufacturing. Similar data for 1960 show the same situation.

However, these data may provide a somewhat inaccurate measure of capital–labor ratios in manufacturing in each state. Creamer's "capital" statistics have limitations.[7] The other measure of capital (profits plus net interest in 1948) is also inadequate. Profit levels in various industries fluctuate differently from year to year. The average profit level over a period of years would be a better indication of the capital stock in each industry. Moreover, any measure of profits provides a very imperfect indication of capital stock, because profits are not necessarily proportional to capital. Rates of return vary greatly from industry to industry.

LABOR INTENSITY AS MEASURED BY VALUE ADDED PER MAN-HOUR (UNADJUSTED)

Another measure of the capital intensity of an industry (or a group of industries) is the value of output produced per man-hour of input. Value added per man-hour should be relatively high in a capital-intensive industry, low in a labor-intensive industry. The logic for this is simple. A man working with a substantial amount of capital equipment can usually produce more value of output each hour than a man who creates a product with his own hands.

The figures in Table 18 show that the differential between value added per man-hour in New England and that in the United States has widened in the postwar period. In 1947, New England's value added per man-hour in manufacturing was 89 per cent of the nation's, and by 1958 it had declined to 83 per cent, remaining at this level in 1963.

This measure of capital intensity suffers from the obvious drawback that labor is not a homogeneous product. A skilled craftsman working with a negligible amount of capital equipment might under some circumstances create as much value each hour as an unskilled man using a $100,000 machine. It is conceivable, therefore, that the level and trend of value added per man-hour in New England could be explained by an increasing use of lower-quality labor inputs. How-

TABLE 18

Value Added by Manufacture per Employee Man-Hour:[a]
*New England Relative to United States Unadjusted and to United States
Adjusted for New England's Industrial Composition*

All Manufacturing
1947, 1954, 1958, and 1963

Year	New England as a Percentage of the United States Unadjusted	New England as a Percentage of the United States Adjusted[b]
1947	89.3	94.2
1954	86.3	93.1
1958	83.2	93.3
1963	83.5	93.7

[a] Man-hours include estimated figures for salaried employees, who are assumed to work 2,000 hours a year.

[b] United States "value added per man-hour" figures adjusted to reflect what average value added per man-hour would be in the nation if the composition of output in the nation were the same as that in New England. See Appendix C for detailed algebraic explanation.

SOURCES: U.S. Bureau of the Census, *Census of Manufactures: 1947* (Washington, D.C.: U.S. Government Printing Office, 1949–1950).

———, *U.S. Census of Manufactures: 1954* (Washington, D.C.: U.S. Government Printing Office, 1957).

———, *U.S. Census of Manufactures: 1958* (Preliminary Reports Series MC[P]) (Washington, D.C.: U.S. Government Printing Office, 1959–1960).

———, *U.S. Census of Manufactures: 1958* (Washington, D.C.: U.S. Government Printing Office, 1961).

———, *Census of Manufactures: 1963* (Preliminary Report Series MC63[P]) (Washington, D.C.: U.S. Government Printing Office, 1965).

———, *Census of Manufactures: 1963* (Industry Statistics Preprints Series MC63[2]) (Washington, D.C.: U.S. Government Printing Office, 1966).

ever, the available labor-skill information as shown in Table 19 does not support this hypothesis.

LABOR INTENSITY AS MEASURED BY VALUE ADDED PER MAN-HOUR (ADJUSTED)

The trend toward labor-intensive specialization in New England might be interpreted in two different ways.

Theory No. 1. It might mean that New England manufacturers were using less capital and more labor to produce the same products as manufacturers in other parts of the country.[8]

TABLE 19

Occupational Distribution of Wage and Salaried Workers in Manufacturing in New England and the United States, 1950 and 1960

Classification of Occupations	New England (Percentage of Employment)		United States (Percentage of Employment)	
	1950	1960	1950	1960
Professional	4.2	6.1	4.5	6.6
Technicians		1.3	.4	1.2
Managerial[a]	2.9	4.1	3.2	4.2
Craftsmen	19.2	20.1	19.9	20.2
Sales	2.0	2.8	3.0	3.9
Clerical	10.8	12.5	11.2	12.3
Bookkeepers	n.a.	.9	1.0	1.0
Cashiers	n.a.	—	.1	.1
Operatives	54.1	48.4	46.8	43.9
Services	1.5	1.3	1.9	1.7
Charwomen, Janitors, Porters	n.a.	.5	.9	.8
Laborers	5.3	3.4	9.0	6.1
TOTAL	100.0[b]	100.0[b]	100.0[b]	100.0[b]

[a] Does not include self-employed.
[b] Detail may not add to total due to rounding.
—: Less than .05%.

SOURCES: U.S. Bureau of the Census, *U.S. Census of Population: 1950.* Vol. II. *Detailed Characteristics* (Washington, D.C.: U.S. Government Printing Office, 1952).

———, *U.S. Census of Population: 1960. Detailed Characteristics.* Connecticut, Maine, Massachusetts, New Hampshire, Rhode Island, and Vermont (separate publication for each state) (Series PC[1]) (Washington, D.C.: U.S. Government Printing Office, 1962), Table 125.

———, *U.S. Census of Population: 1960. Supplementary Reports. Industry Group by Occupation: 1960* (Series PC[S1]–27) (Washington, D.C.: U.S. Government Printing Office, 1962).

This theory is diagramed in Figure 4. This diagram is unusual in that the customary isoquant lines are replaced by iso–value-added lines. Line $P_{U.S.}$–$P_{U.S.}$ represents the various combinations of capital and labor which can be used by manufacturers in the United States to produce a given amount of value added of a given product. Line $P_{N.E.}$–$P_{N.E.}$ shows that manufacturers in New England must combine more labor and capital to produce the same amount of value added of

FIGURE 4
THEORY NO. 1
Manufacturing in New England and the United States

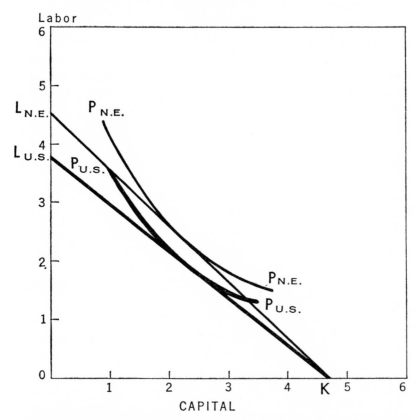

$P_{N.E.}$–$P_{N.E.}$: Possible combinations of productive factors for a given amount of value added of a product in New England.

$P_{U.S.}$–$P_{U.S.}$: Possible combinations of productive factors for a given amount of value added (the same amount as in New England) of a product in the United States.

The slope of line $L_{N.E.}$–K represents the relative cost of labor and capital in New England.

The slope of line $L_{U.S.}$–K represents the relative cost of labor and capital in the United States.

the same product. This is true because the region's producers are distant from raw materials and national markets. Because of low wage rates in their region, New England manufacturers would be expected to use relatively more labor than manufacturers in the United States. In this diagram lines $P_{U.S.}-P_{U.S.}$ and $P_{N.E.}-P_{N.E.}$ are drawn to indicate that labor can be easily substituted for capital in the production process.

Theory No. 2. The trend toward labor-intensive specialization in New England might also be interpreted to mean that New England manufacturers specialize in products requiring a labor-intensive technology. In this case, New England firms could be using the same technology as their counterparts when they produce identical products. However, they would tend to produce different products. They would specialize in items manufactured with a technology requiring the use of a considerable amount of human effort per unit of output.

This theory is diagramed in Figure 5. In this diagram two different types of products are considered. Product *A* is the type of product manufactured with labor-intensive techniques. Product *B* is typical of goods manufactured with capital-intensive techniques. In both cases the assumption is made that it is difficult to substitute labor for capital and vice versa. Hence, the iso–value-added lines are steeply curved.

As shown in this diagram, New England manufacturers would have great difficulty competing with United States manufacturers in *B* types of products. The region's locational disadvantage is represented by the substantial distance between $P_{U.S.}^{B}-P_{U.S.}^{B}$ and $P_{N.E.}^{B}-P_{N.E.}^{B}$. Capital-intensive products typically require the processing of large amounts of raw material and the use of large amounts of fuel and electrical energy. Furthermore, the final product may be bulky and heavy and therefore expensive to ship to national markets. On the other hand, New England locational disadvantages are much less important in *A* types of products, where substantial human effort is devoted to a small volume of raw materials.

Which of these two theories best explains the New England situation? Table 20 shows that Theory 2 provides the greater part of the explanation. In 1958 and 1963, about 65 per cent of the difference between value added per man-hour in the nation and that in New England was eliminated by adjusting the United States figures for

FIGURE 5

THEORY No. 2

Manufacturing in New England and the United States

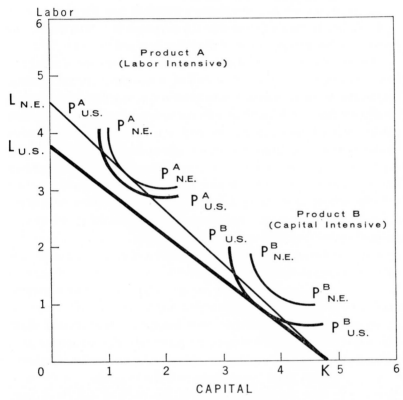

$PA_{N.E.}-PA_{N.E.}$: Possible combinations of productive factors for a given amount of value added of Product *A* in New England.

$PA_{U.S.}-PA_{U.S.}$: Possible combinations of productive factors for a given amount of value added (the same amount as in New England) of Product *A* in the United States.

$\left.\begin{array}{l} PB_{N.E.}-PB_{N.E.} \\ PB_{U.S.}-PB_{U.S.} \end{array}\right\}$ The same as above for Product *B*.

The slope of line $L_{N.E.}-K$ represents the relative cost of labor and capital in New England.

The slope of line $L_{U.S.}-K$ represents the relative cost of labor and capital in the United States.

New England's product mix. This adjustment was made by calculating what value added per man-hour in all manufacturing in the United States would be if the nation had the same three- and four-digit industry mix as New England.

However, this 65 per cent figure is probably low, for two reasons.

First, the measure—value added per man-hour—exaggerates the physical output per man-hour differential between New England and the United States. A given dollar of value added in New England is likely to represent more physical output than a dollar of value added in the nation. Value added by manufacture is the difference between the selling price (f.o.b. mill) of a manufacturer's final product and the cost of raw materials, energy, fuel, and other purchased items used in the manufacturing process. In New England, manufacturers typically receive less for their products (f.o.b. mill) and pay more for their raw materials (delivered at the mill) because they are located farther from markets and sources of raw material than are their counterparts in the nation. As a result, they create less value added per unit of physical output than their national competitors.

Second, the adjustment process is imperfect. For example, the adjusted figure for the two-digit paper and allied products industry in the United States suggests that it has a greater concentration of relatively labor-intensive three- and four-digit subindustries than its counterpart two-digit industry in New England. The reverse is probably true. New England manufacturers produce fine writing papers, book papers, technical papers, and specialty papers of all sorts. These products require a more labor-intensive technology than do the kraft papers and other standardized papers produced in the South and West. The reason the adjustment process did not work in this case is that over 40 per cent of New England's output in the two-digit "Paper and Allied Products" industry comes from one three-digit industry, "Paper-Mill Products." "Paper-Mill Products" is not broken down into four-digit subindustries. This is unfortunate because New England paper-mill products are manufactured with a different technology from similarly classified products in the nation.

For these two reasons it is possible to estimate that at least two-thirds of the differential between New England and the United States are accounted for by the labor-intensive product mix of the region's manufacturing firms.

How can the remaining one-third be explained? Theory No. 1 is

TABLE 20

Value Added by Manufacture per Employee Man-Hour.[a] New England, United States Unadjusted, and United States Adjusted for New England's Industrial Composition

All Manufacturing

1947, 1954, 1958, and 1963

Year	New England	United States	United States Adjusted[b]	United States Minus New England	United States Minus United States Adjusted	Percentage of the Differential Between New England and the United States Explained by New England's Specialization in Labor-Intensive Products
1947	$2.26	$2.53	$2.40	$ .27	$ .13	48.1
1954	3.22	3.73	3.46	.51	.27	52.9
1958	3.90	4.69	4.18	.79	.51	64.6
1963	4.90	5.87	5.23	.97	.64	66.0

[a] Man-hours include estimated figures for salaried employees, who are assumed to work 2,000 hours a year.

[b] See footnote b to Table 18 and Appendix C.

SOURCES: U.S. Bureau of the Census, Census of Manufactures: 1947 (Washington, D.C.: U.S. Government Printing Office, 1949–1950).

————, U.S. Census of Manufactures: 1954 (Washington, D.C.: U.S. Government Printing Office, 1957).

————, U.S. Census of Manufactures: 1958 (Preliminary Reports Series MC[P]) (Washington, D.C.: U.S. Government Printing Office, 1959–1960).

————, U.S. Census of Manufactures: 1958 (Washington, D.C.: U.S. Government Printing Office, 1961).

————, Census of Manufactures: 1963 (Preliminary Reports Series MC63[P]) (Washington, D.C.: U.S. Government Printing Office, 1965).

————, Census of Manufactures: 1963 (Industry Statistics Preprints Series MC63[2]) (Washington, D.C.: U.S. Government Printing Office, 1966).

useful. Some manufacturing firms in New England consciously minimize costs by depending more on the services of labor and less on the
services of capital because labor can be purchased at a lower cost in
New England. Some firms, because of insufficient profits, are unable
to finance new buildings and equipment. Still other manufacturing
firms in New England continue to use old equipment long after the
same machinery has been abandoned in other parts of the country
because they are unaware of or uninterested in new equipment. Unfortunately, no reliable data are available to gauge accurately the relative importance of each of these reasons.

Does the broad generalization that New England produces more
labor-intensive products than the United States hold true in all industries? There is one obvious exception. The textile industry is clearly
more capital-intensive in New England than in the United States.
This is logical because wage rates in this industry are substantially
higher in New England than in the South.

What is surprising, perhaps, is that the textile industry has declined so rapidly in New England in the postwar period, since this
industry is inherently labor-intensive. In 1947 the region's textile employment comprised 18.1 per cent of the total manufacturing labor
force, and by 1964 this percentage had declined to 7.0 per cent. It
should be remembered, however, that the textile industry depends on
unskilled labor, which is plentiful in southern states but is in relatively
short supply in New England.

On the other hand, rapid industrial growth in New England in
the postwar period has taken place in light metalworking industries.
There also has been fast growth in research-and-development-oriented
manufacturing. These types of manufacturing are the ultimate in
labor-intensive production, because they do not depend heavily on
imported raw material and do not result in a heavy or bulky product
with high shipping costs per unit of output.

LABOR INTENSITY AS MEASURED BY VALUE ADDED PER DOLLAR OF
WAGES

Although the "value added per man-hour" figure provides a good
indication of the labor intensity of all manufacturing in New England,
it can be a misleading indicator for individual industries within manufacturing. If the skill level of an industry is high (for example, trans-

portation equipment and machinery), the output per man-hour is necessarily much greater than in low-skill industries (such as textiles, apparel, leather and shoes). However, high-skill industries are not necessarily capital-intensive. The aircraft industry (one of the three-digit components of the two-digit transportation equipment industry) has relatively high value added per man-hour but is generally accepted as being labor-intensive because wage and salary payments comprise a large fraction of value added by manufacture.[9]

Table 21 shows the relative importance of the components of value added by manufacture in all manufacturing in the United States as of 1957. These components can be divided into three categories: (*a*) payments for the services of labor at the plant level (55.8 per cent), (*b*) payments for the services of capital (21.5 per cent), and (*c*) other expenses (22.7 per cent). Many of these "other expenses" (for example, payrolls and payroll supplements at central administrative offices and auxiliary plants, contract research, royalty payments, advertising, publicity, legal services) are overhead items allocated at head offices to individual manufacturing plants. Thus, the ratio of value added to wage and salary payments is a measure of the relative importance of plant payroll costs. It is a reasonably good indicator of the labor intensity of individual manufacturing industries in the United States.

This ratio is sometimes deficient, however, when used to compare total manufacturing in a region with total manufacturing in the United States. Labor-intensive industries are generally concentrated in low-wage regions. In such regions, a given amount of wage and salary payments will buy more labor services than in a high-wage region. As a result, the ratio of wage and salary payments to value added tends to underestimate the relative importance of labor services in a region such as New England. Table 22 shows that for all manufacturing in New England (on both an unadjusted and an adjusted basis) the percentage gap between New England and the United States is considerably less when measured by the ratio of value added to wage and salary payments than when measured by the ratio of value added to man-hours (Table 18). The inherent bias in wage and salary statistics could be corrected if there were measures of the regional variation in the price of labor. Unfortunately no aggregate regional labor-price indices for manufacturing are available.

TABLE 21

Components of Value Added by Manufacture in the United States, 1957

Component	Amount (in billions of dollars)	Percentage of Total Value Added
1. Payroll of operating establishments	76.4	51.7
2. Supplements to payroll of operating establishments	6.0	4.1
A. TOTAL DIRECT COST OF LABOR	82.4	55.8
3. Depreciation	7.3	4.9
4. Corporate profits (before taxes), proprietors' income (before taxes), net interest paid	24.6[a]	16.6
B. TOTAL PAYMENTS FOR SERVICE OF CAPITAL (BEFORE TAXES)	31.9	21.5
5. Taxes on land, structures, equipment, inventories	1.5	1.0
6. Maintenance and repair services purchased from other firms	4.5	3.0
7. Insurance	.7	.5
8. Payroll in central administrative offices and auxiliary establishments	4.2	2.9
9. Miscellaneous expenses		
These include excise taxes, sales taxes, permit fees, supplements to payroll at central administrative office and auxiliary establishments, travel and communication expenses, entertainment expenses, and bad debts. They also include numerous company-type expenses which can not be reported on an establishment basis by multiestablishment firms. Examples are advertising, publicity, legal services, royalty payments, and contract research.	22.6	15.3
C. TOTAL OTHER EXPENSES	33.5	22.7
TOTAL VALUE ADDED BY MANUFACTURE	147.8	100.0

[a] This figure taken from the National Income Accounts as estimated by National Income Division, Office of Business Economics, U.S. Department of Commerce. It is a good approximation but is not entirely comparable with other figures in the table taken from the Census of Manufactures.

SOURCE: U.S. Bureau of the Census, *U.S. Census of Manufactures: 1958.* Vol. I. *Summary Statistics* (Washington, D.C.: U.S. Government Printing Office, 1961), pp. 12-14 and pp. 8-2, 8-7.

TABLE 22

Ratio of Value Added by Manufacture to Total Wages and Salaries:
New England Relative to United States Unadjusted and to United States
Adjusted for New England's Industrial Composition

All Manufacturing
1947, 1954, 1958, and 1963

Year	New England Ratio as a Percentage of United States Ratio Unadjusted	New England Ratio as a Percentage of United States Ratio Adjusted[a]
1947	94.3	96.7
1954	93.4	96.3
1958	90.1	96.6
1963	88.9	96.4

[a] United States ratio adjusted so as to reflect what the ratio of value added to total wages and salaries would be in the nation if the composition of output in the nation were the same as that in New England.

SOURCES: U.S. Bureau of the Census, *Census of Manufactures: 1947* (Washington, D.C.: U.S. Government Printing Office, 1949–1950).

————, *U.S. Census of Manufactures: 1954* (Washington, D.C.: U.S. Government Printing Office, 1957).

————, *U.S. Census of Manufactures: 1958* (Preliminary Reports Series MC[P]) (Washington, D.C.: U.S. Government Printing Office, 1959–1960).

————, *U.S. Census of Manufactures: 1958* (Washington, D.C.: U.S. Government Printing Office, 1961).

————, *Census of Manufactures: 1963* (Preliminary Reports Series MC63 [P]) (Washington, D.C.: U.S. Government Printing Office, 1965).

————, *Census of Manufactures: 1963* (Industry Statistics Preprints Series MC63[2]) (Washington, D.C.: U.S. Government Printing Office, 1966).

PERCENTAGE OF EMPLOYMENT IN LABOR-INTENSIVE INDUSTRIES

Another way of measuring labor intensity is to classify each three-digit industry in the United States as labor-intensive or capital-intensive, depending on whether wage and salary payments as a percentage of value added are above or below the national average for all manufacturing. In 1954 the national average was 52.2 per cent; in 1947 it was 53.4 per cent. Then the percentage of employment in labor-intensive three-digit industries can be calculated for each region. Table 23 shows that New England has predominantly labor-intensive manufacturing. It also shows that in the 1947–1958 period New England manufacturers increasingly specialized in labor-intensive production.

TABLE 23
*Percentage of Total Manufacturing Employment
in the Labor-Intensive Industries*[a]

Region	1947	1958
New England	74.7	77.3
Middle Atlantic	72.8	64.3
East North Central	81.4	54.5
West North Central	67.6	63.4
South Atlantic	49.1	69.9
East South Central	56.4	63.3
West South Central	41.0	57.0
Mountain	40.4	58.7
Pacific	58.4	70.9
UNITED STATES	69.2	63.6

[a] Labor-intensive industries defined as those three-digit industries in which total wage and salary payments equaled a greater percentage of value added for the industry than the corresponding percentage for all manufacturing in the United States.

SOURCES: U.S. Bureau of the Census, *U.S. Census of Manufactures: 1954* (Washington, D.C.: U.S. Government Printing Office, 1957).

————, *U.S. Census of Manufactures: 1958* (Washington, D.C.: U.S. Government Printing Office, 1961).

BOOK VALUE OF ASSETS PER EMPLOYEE

Table 24 shows that 86 per cent of New England's manufacturing employment is in four-digit industries which have below national average gross and net book value of depreciable or depletable assets per employee. In the nation, 75 per cent of manufacturing employment is in such labor-intensive industries.

Figure 6 and Table 25 show that capital-intensive industries in New England tend to be clustered just above the national average for gross book value per employee. Similarly, a large fraction of the labor-intensive industries is well below the national average. The data on *net* book value per employee have an almost identical relationship and are, therefore, not shown.

"Capital-Intensive" Labor

This chapter has shown that New England's manufacturers specialize in labor-intensive products. These products have been classified as "labor-intensive" because a relatively large number of man-hours is required for each dollar of value added by manufacturing. As a

TABLE 24

Employment in New England and the United States in Selected Capital-Intensive and Labor-Intensive Four-Digit Industries,[a] 1947 and 1958

	New England				United States	
	1947 Employment	Percentage of Total in Industries Studied	1958 Employment	Percentage of Total in Industries Studied	1958 Employment[b]	Percentage of Total in Industries Studied
On Basis of *Gross* Book Value 12/31/57 of Depreciable Assets per Employee						
Capital-Intensive	194,708	15.2	165,429	14.4	3,417,000	25.0
Labor-Intensive	1,084,540	84.8	985,826	85.6	10,262,000	75.0
TOTAL	1,279,248	100.0	1,151,255	100.0	13,679,000	100.0
On Basis of *Net* Book Value 12/31/57 of Depreciable Assets per Employee[c]						
Capital-Intensive	194,914	15.2	158,142	13.7	3,345,000	24.5
Labor-Intensive	1,084,334	84.8	993,113	86.3	10,334,000	75.5
TOTAL	1,279,248	100.0	1,151,255	100.0	13,679,000	100.0

a Four-digit industries for which individual data are available. Employment equals 86.7 per cent of total manufacturing employment in New England in 1947, 84.7 per cent in 1958, and 88.1 per cent in the United States in 1958.
b Capital-intensive industry defined as one with gross book value of depreciable or depletable assets per employee above the average for all manufacturing in the United States in 1958 ($7,110 per employee).
c Capital-intensive industry defined as one with net book value of depreciable or depletable assets per employee above the average for all manufacturing in the United States in 1958 ($3.53 per employee).

SOURCES: U.S. Bureau of the Census, *Census of Manufactures: 1947.* Vol. II. *Statistics by Industry* (Washington, D.C.: U.S. Government Printing Office, 1949).

———, *U.S. Census of Manufactures: 1954.* Vol. III. *Area Statistics* (Washington, D.C.: U.S. Government Printing Office, 1957).

———, *U.S. Census of Manufactures: 1958* (Preliminary Reports Series MC[P]) (Washington, D.C.: U.S. Government Printing Office, 1959–1960).

———, *U.S. Census of Manufactures: 1958.* Vol. I. *Summary Statistics* (Washington, D.C.: U.S. Government Printing Office, 1961), pp. 9-8–9-23.

FIGURE 6

Percentage of Manufacturing Employment in Industries Ranged By Gross Book Value Per Employee of Depreciable or Depletable Assets

New England and the United States

December 31, 1957

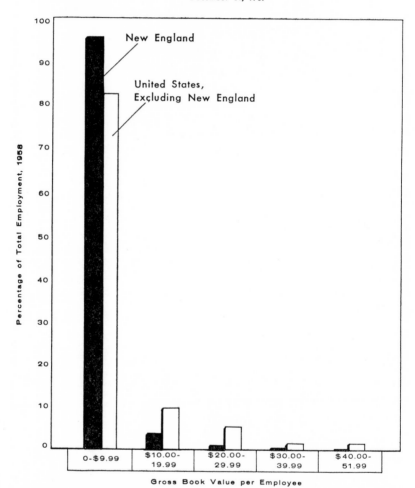

Gross Book Value per Employee

Source: U.S. Bureau of the Census, *U.S. Census of Manufactures: 1958.* Vol. I. *Summary Statistics* (Washington, D.C.: U.S. Government Printing Office, 1961), Table 1.

TABLE 25

*Distribution of 1958 Manufacturing Employment in New England
and in the Rest of the United States:
Industries Ranged by Gross Book Value per Employee
of Depreciable or Depletable Assets
as of December 31, 1957*

	Gross Book Value of Assets per Employee ($000)	New England		Rest of United States	
		Employment	Percentage of Total	Employment	Percentage of Total
1st quartile (U.S. = 25% of total employment)	$0.00– 3.39	314,230	27.3	3,136,770	25.0
2nd quartile (U.S. = 25%)	3.40– 5.46	382,790	33.2	3,165,210	25.3
3rd quartile (U.S. = 25%)	5.47– 7.44	303,778	26.4	3,127,222	25.0
4th quartile (U.S. = 25%)	7.45–51.69	150,457	13.1	3,098,543	24.7
TOTAL[a]		1,151,255	100.0	12,527,745	100.0

[a] Total employment in four-digit industries for which individual data are available. Employment totals shown here equal 84.7 per cent of total manufacturing employment in New England, 88.45 per cent in the rest of the United States, and 88.1 per cent in the United States.

SOURCES: U.S. Bureau of the Census, *U.S. Census of Manufactures: 1958* (Preliminary Reports Series MC[P]) (Washington, D.C.: U.S. Government Printing Office, 1959–1960).

———, *U.S. Census of Manufactures: 1958.* Vol. I. *Summary Statistics* (Washington, D.C.: U.S. Government Printing Office, 1961), pp. 9-8–9-23.

result, wage and salary payments constitute an unusually large portion of value added. In addition, these products generally require smaller amounts of raw materials, industrial fuel, electrical energy, and capital equipment than the average for all products manufactured in the nation.

However, many of the new labor-intensive industries in New England require large numbers of highly skilled workers, technicians, and engineers. These workers must be trained at considerable expense in public or private schools and on the job. Their education involves a substantial capital investment which is paid for by the public, by private philanthropy, by their employers, and by the individuals themselves. In a sense, therefore, the new high-skill industries in New England require a capital-intensive type of labor.

Chapter VII

ADVANTAGES OF THE HEAD START

N EW England has had the advantage of a "head start." The region had a large concentration of population and an industrialized economy in the nineteenth century at a time when most other regions in the country were oriented to agriculture.

Chapter V has shown how this "head start" has helped maintain population growth in the twentieth century. Although a significant number of native-born persons have moved from New England, this out-migration has been overwhelmed by the natural population increase and the in-migration of the foreign-born. The net result has been a continuous population growth in almost every New England state in every decade since 1870. This population growth has continued even though many workers could have found jobs paying 5 to 15 per cent more if they had moved to other parts of the United States. New England's migration history suggests that wage differentials of this magnitude will not induce substantial interregional migration. For this reason, historical concentrations of population in disadvantaged regions are maintained from decade to decade.

The following sections explain how New England's early "head start" has provided the region with other competitive advantages which have helped maintain its growth momentum throughout the twentieth century.

The Goals of Management

Most manufacturing firms in New England are managed by men who were born and raised in the region where their manufacturing facilities are located. Unless their firms are failing, these men do not consider relocating to improve their profit position. Ellis[1] and Wickman[2] have shown that the typical executive instinctively prefers to operate his firm in a familiar environment.

THE ELLIS SURVEY

Ellis interviewed the executives of 106 manufacturing establishments which began operations in New England between August 1945, and June 1948. Of the total, 42 were new firms, 44 were branch plants of existing firms, and 20 were relocations of manufacturing operations from outside the region. Ellis found that in the large majority of cases, personal considerations and/or production linkages with existing New England manufacturing facilities dominated the location decision.

In 29 of the 42 new firms, the "president or partners who organized the new firms desired to maintain their established residences, or they were personally acquainted with a few workers who served as the nucleus of their work force, or they were personally acquainted with some local jobbers who furnished initial markets."[3]

Of the 44 branch plants, personal considerations were dominant in only two cases. In another 18 cases, however, the branch plant was set up "to perform a step in the production process which started or ended in the parent plant" which was located in New England.

Personal considerations dominated the decision in 6 of the 20 relocation cases.

THE WICKMAN SURVEY

In 1961 Wickman sent mail questionnaires to 227 wood-furniture manufacturers in New England. Only 60 usable questionnaires were returned. However, these replies provided substantial information regarding the following questions:[4]

1. *"What are the locational advantages and disadvantages of a New England location?"*

The large majority of manufacturers stated that transportation costs, labor costs, and taxes were relatively high in New England. On the other hand, they praised the "good educational and recreational facilities" and the "good cultural and social environment."

The survey showed that most furniture manufacturers believe New England is a high-cost area. The detailed data in other parts of Wickman's thesis tend to support this judgment.

2. *"Do you anticipate a move to a new location in the foreseeable future?"*

Only 7 of 53 respondents were considering a move to a new location. Five of the 7 were planning to relocate *within* New England.

3. *"Is your company at its original location?"*

Of 58 respondents, 35 stated that their firms were at the original location. Those that had relocated had moved within the same town or to a nearby town.

4. *"If you were founding a new furniture manufacturing company this year or building a brand-new plant for your present company, and had the financial resources to relocate anywhere in the United States, where would you choose to locate?"*

Of 52 respondents, 21 thought of locating outside the region. Most of the 21 preferred the South.

5. *"Why did your company locate where it is today?"*

It is difficult to analyze the replies to this question because many managers did not know what motivated the founders of their firms. However, the survey results suggest that personal considerations played an important role. Locational factors such as low labor costs, low material costs, and proximity to markets were rarely mentioned.

Questionnaire returns are notoriously inaccurate and difficult to analyze. Nevertheless, Wickman's study strongly suggests that small manufacturers are emotionally linked to their present location and rarely think of relocating in other regions to improve their profit position.

OTHER STUDIES

Numerous other studies have shown that personal considerations may determine the original location of a plant. The studies also show that once established, manufacturing facilities are rarely moved to another region.

Hunter[5] has described this type of historical development for the paper industry in New England. Miernyk has shown that numerous northern firms in the cotton textile industry,[6] in the woolen and worsted industry,[7] and in the shoe industry[8] deliberately chose to remain in high-cost locations. In a Michigan study, Katona and Morgan[9] found that personal considerations influenced the location decisions of manufacturing executives in a variety of industries. In a study of eight plant-location decisions in Alabama, Greenhut[10] found that personal considerations prevailed in five cases.

None of these studies invalidates the traditional ideas of location theory. Executives are interested in profits. It appears, however, that most executives are willing to accept a somewhat lower rate of return for the privilege of operating in a familiar environment.

In many types of manufacturing, costs of materials, transportation, and other factors are extremely important. In these industries, executives have little freedom in choosing plant locations. It was demonstrated in Chapters II and VI, however, that New England firms are not tied to raw materials, industrial fuels, electric power, or national consumer markets. Many New England firms could operate equally well in a great variety of locations. Lower labor costs and a familiar environment encourage indigenous manufacturing firms to remain in the region.

The Composition of Economic Activity

As an industrial society develops, it generally becomes less dependent on industries based on natural resources. With efficient equipment and modern technology, a much smaller proportion of the population is needed in farming, forestry, fishing, and mining. Gradually a substantial portion of the labor force is freed to work in the rapidly growing manufacturing sector. When industrial development produces a very high level of per capita income, the growth rate in manufacturing usually declines and the growth rate in service industries accelerates.[11]

Both the New England and the United States economies have moved through each of these stages of growth. At each step, however, New England's development has preceded that of the nation. In 1870, for example, 44 per cent of the labor force in New England were employed in manufacturing, compared to 21 per cent in the nation. In the same year 26 per cent of the region's labor force and 51 per cent of the nation's were engaged in agricultural pursuits. Subsequently, between 1870 and 1910, rapidly growing demands for manufactured products brought about a 300 per cent increase in the nation's manufacturing employment. Agricultural employment increased only 92 per cent.

As a result of the region's geographical handicaps, New England's manufacturing employment increased only 150 per cent from 1870 to 1910. About 877,000 fewer persons were employed in manufacturing in New England in 1910 than would have been if employment in manufacturing in each New England state had increased at the national rate during this period.[12] Nevertheless, New England's over-all growth was much faster than it would have been if the region had not benefited from a favorable composition of economic activity at the beginning of the period.

New England's early specialization in certain types of service industries has also helped maintain growth. During the last two decades, rapidly increasing real per capita earnings in the United States have stimulated a growing demand for the output of insurance companies,[13] vacation businesses,[14] research and development laboratories, private educational institutions,[15] and hospitals. These are all important employers in New England. They are also net exporters; that is, persons and firms in other regions buy more insurance, vacation, hospital, and education services in New England than New Englanders buy in other regions. As of 1951, the research, development, and business services industry and the hospital industry were not among the top fifteen export industries in Massachusetts. By 1962 they ranked fifth and seventh respectively, while private colleges and universities moved up from seventh to third place.[16] These are all labor-intensive industries which rely on a plentiful supply of skilled labor.

The Growth of Nearby Markets

Even though New England producers have generally lost position in national markets, they often remain competitive in the markets of adjoining regions. For example, manufacturing employment in the United States continues to be concentrated in the area north of the Mason-Dixon line and east of the Mississippi River. As a result, the market for producers' durable goods is concentrated in the same area, as shown in Table 26. When New England manufacturers of producers' durable goods ship into this market, they have a minor transportation cost disadvantage vis-à-vis producers in the Midwest. Table 27 shows that 19 per cent of New England's manufacturing employment produces durable goods for manufacturing industries. In the nation, only 12 per cent of the manufacturing employment is in this type of industry.

TABLE 26

Percentage of United States Population, Personal Income, and Manufacturing Activity Located in the Northeastern United States, 1960

Area	Population	Personal Income	Total Manufacturing Employment	Value Added in Manufacturing	Expenditures for Plant and Equipment by Manufacturing Establishments in Operation	
					New Structures and Additions to Plant	New Machinery and Equipment
New England (Maine, N.H., Vt., Mass., R.I., Conn.)	5.9	6.5	9.1	7.5	5.2	6.6
Middle Atlantic (N.Y., N.J., Pa.)	19.0	22.2	26.2	24.2	19.9	21.1
East North Central (Ohio, Ind., Ill., Mich., Wis.)	20.2	21.6	27.9	29.6	28.9	29.9
Part of South Atlantic (Del., Md.)	2.0	2.2	1.9	2.0	2.0	2.0
NORTHEASTERN UNITED STATES	47.1	52.5	65.1	63.3	56.0	59.6

SOURCES: U.S. Bureau of the Census, *U.S. Census of Population: 1960.* Vol. I. *Characteristics of the Population. Part A. Number of Inhabitants* (Washington, D.C.: U.S. Government Printing Office, 1961), Table 9.

——, *Annual Survey of Manufactures: 1960* (Series M60[AS]-1, -6, -4.1, -4.2, -4.3, -4.5) (Washington, D.C.: U.S. Government Printing Office, 1962).

Edwin J. Coleman, "Personal Income by States in 1961," *Survey of Current Business*, XLII (August, 1962), 12–16.

TABLE 27

Estimated Percentage of Manufacturing Employment in New England and the United States Devoted to Production of Manufacturers' Durables, 1947 and 1958

| | 1947 | | | | 1958 | | | |
| | New England | | United States | | New England | | United States | |
Industry	Employment	Percentage of Total	Employment	Percentage of Total	Employment	Percentage of Total	Employment	Percentage of Total
Blast furnaces & steel mills[a]	1,197	0.1	127,981	0.9	901	0.1	121,711	0.8
Steel wire drawing[a]	826	0.1	4,838	—	1,352	0.1	4,582	—
Cold finishing of steel shapes[a]	—	—	—	—	402	—	2,604	—
Steel pipes & tubes	20	—	3,128	—	20	—	5,691	—
Nonferrous wire drawing, etc.	17,885	1.2	14,754	0.1	15,174	1.1	56,493	0.4
Edge tools	11,438	0.8	48,942	0.3	6,265	0.5	30,273	0.2
Hand saws & saw blades	2,787	0.2	8,441	0.1	1,921	0.1	5,509	—
Screw-machine prod. & bolts	15,520	1.1	77,727	0.5	14,764	1.1	85,106	0.6
Fabricated metal prod. n.e.c.	10,429	0.7	126,105	0.9	14,255	1.0	137,333	0.9
Engines & turbines	9,552	0.6	93,064	0.6	9,378	0.7	95,572	0.6

See footnotes at end of table.

TABLE 27 (*continued*)

Industry	1947 NEW ENGLAND Employment	1947 NEW ENGLAND Percentage of Total	1947 UNITED STATES Employment	1947 UNITED STATES Percentage of Total	1958 NEW ENGLAND Employment	1958 NEW ENGLAND Percentage of Total	1958 UNITED STATES Employment	1958 UNITED STATES Percentage of Total
Metalworking machinery	27,252	1.8	127,442	0.9	38,889	2.8	233,523	1.5
Special industrial machinery	53,624	3.6	137,288	1.0	33,528	2.5	162,262	1.1
General industrial machinery	34,324	2.3	200,385	1.4	32,825	2.4	211,382	1.4
Machine shops	4,788	0.3	58,160	0.4	9,365	0.7	115,535	0.8
Electric measuring instruments	6,068	0.4	20,926	0.1	7,991	0.6	46,923	0.3
Transformers	10,645	0.7	36,635	0.3	6,630	0.5	34,601	0.2
Switchgear & switchboards	b	—	b	—	5,296	0.4	52,871	0.4
Electric industrial apparatus	16,135	1.1	225,424	1.6	6,374	0.5	156,332	1.0
Electric lamps	3,667	0.3	23,842	0.2	2,607	0.2	21,495	0.1
Current-carrying devices	11,319	0.8	38,367	0.3	11,366	0.8	34,808	0.2
Noncurrent-carrying devices	c	—	c		913	0.1	19,722	0.1

See footnotes at end of table.

TABLE 27 (continued)

Industry	1947				1958			
	NEW ENGLAND		UNITED STATES		NEW ENGLAND		UNITED STATES	
	Employ-ment	Percentage of Total	Employ-ment	Percentage of Total	Employ-ment	Percentage of Total	Employ-ment	Percentage of Total
Electronic components	6,182	0.4	56,532	0.4	25,851	1.9	132,242	0.9
Mechanical measuring devices	8,481	0.6	53,237	0.4	14,750	1.1	75,562	0.5
TOTAL, MANUFAC-TURERS' DUR-ABLES	252,139	17.1	1,483,218	10.4	260,817	19.2	1,842,132	12.0
TOTAL, ALL INDUSTRIES	1,474,684		14,294,304		1,359,919		15,393,766	

a Proportion of employment in the industry estimated to be devoted to production of manufacturers' durable goods.
b Included under electrical industrial apparatus.
c Included under current-carrying devices.
SOURCES: Board of Governors of the Federal Reserve System, Industrial Production: 1959 Revision (Washington, D.C.: The Board, 1960).
U.S. Bureau of the Census, Census of Manufactures: 1947. Vol. II. Statistics by Industry (Washington, D.C.: U.S. Government Printing Office, 1949).
———, Census of Manufactures: 1947. Vol. III. Statistics by States (Washington, D.C.: U.S. Government Printing Office, 1950).
———, U.S. Census of Manufactures: 1954. Vol. III. Area Statistics (Washington, D.C.: U.S. Government Printing Office, 1957).
———, U.S. Census of Manufactures: 1958. Vol. III. Area Statistics (Washington, D.C.: U.S. Government Printing Office, 1961).

Defense Spending

New England's competitive position was improved by technological changes introduced during World War II. During the war the federal government placed substantial military contracts with metalworking firms and with research organizations throughout New England. When the region's firms and institutions helped develop the new weaponry, they were forced to use new production techniques and to become familiar with entirely new technologies. This experience enabled them to grow rapidly in the postwar period. It also induced a structural shift in the economy. In 1939 metalworking industries accounted for 28 per cent of the region's manufacturing employment. In 1947 metalworking employment accounted for 38 per cent of the manufacturing jobs.[17]

Agglomeration Economies

Except for the Middle Atlantic states, no other region has as large a proportion of its population living in concentrated groups. Almost 61 per cent of the population in New England live in urbanized areas, and 71 per cent live in standard metropolitan areas. In the rest of the United States, 53 per cent live in urbanized areas and 62 per cent live in metropolitan areas.

Figure 7 shows that almost all the land area in Massachusetts, Connecticut, and Rhode Island is within twenty miles of a standard metropolitan statistical area. Furthermore, much of the population in New Hampshire and Maine is within twenty miles of the metropolitan areas of Manchester, New Hampshire, Portland, Maine, and Lewiston–Auburn, Maine. In all, 87.6 per cent of the population in New England are within easy commuting distance of an officially designated metropolitan area.

A manufacturer establishing a new plant in a large metropolitan area has many advantages over an employer setting up a plant in a rural area. A skilled labor force can be recruited in the vicinity, and public and private vocational schools are already established to train high school students and adults for skilled jobs. Specialized government services such as libraries and industrial waste-disposal facilities may also be available.

What is unique about New England is that each of its metropolitan areas is within a six-hour drive of the others. Thus, specialized manu-

FIGURE 7

*Standard Metropolitan Statistical Areas and Surrounding
20-Mile Area, New England*

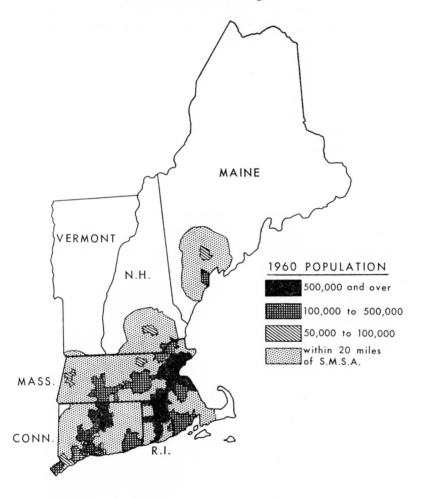

SOURCE: U.S. Bureau of the Census, *U.S. Census of Population: 1960*
(Washington, D.C.: U.S. Government Printing Office, 1961).

facturers and suppliers of parts, expert repairmen, and industrial consultants in one metropolitan area are within easy reach of any manufacturer in New England. The availability of this type of supporting service is very important in some industries. Easterlin has suggested that external economies are important for firms in the primary metals, fabricated metals, electrical machinery, nonelectrical machinery, and transportation equipment industries.[18] These are the growing industries in New England, and they now account for 40 per cent of total manufacturing employment.

Chapter VIII

CONCLUSIONS AND IMPLICATIONS

R ELATIVELY low wage rates and substantial unemployment have not induced a large out-migration from New England. The natural increase in population plus foreign in-migration far exceeds the net out-migration of native-born persons. As a result, the labor supply increases in each New England state each year.

The response to wage differentials is sluggish in all parts of the country. Older workers are reluctant to leave secure positions and familiar surroundings. Younger workers are unwilling to move long distances unless they are assured of jobs with much higher earnings. Sjaastad[1] has suggested that, in most states, the personal income would have to drop to a level 50 per cent below the national average before out-migration would exceed the natural population increase.

This book has shown that the average manufacturing wage in New England diverged downward from the national average between 1947 and 1960. It has also shown that wage differentials amounting to 15 per cent or more for identical work continue to exist between New England labor markets only one hundred miles apart. The wage differences are maintained because of the differential growth of employment opportunities in different labor markets and because employees in every labor market respond sluggishly to job opportunities in outside labor markets. The textile cities with declining employment in manufacturing have lower relative wage rates. The labor markets with the fast-growing metalworking industries (such as Hartford) maintain wage levels approaching the national average.

In addition to the advantage provided by the region's relatively low wage rates, manufacturers in New England benefit from external economies resulting from the aggregation of eighteeen metropolitan areas within three hundred miles of each other. On the other hand, costs of raw materials, transportation to national consumer markets, fuel, electricity, construction and the cost of living are higher in New England than elsewhere. In addition, the soil resources of the region are poor.

Thus, New England has few unique locational advantages and many significant disadvantages. It is a historical accident that the region is an important population and manufacturing center. As a result, the typical New England manufacturer generally is forced to produce for a local or regional market or to specialize in products which must be manufactured with a high-skill, labor-intensive technique.

The evidence presented in this book suggests that most new employment opportunities in the region arise from the expansion of firms already established there or the creation of new firms by New England executives who prefer to remain where they are. Thus, while low wage rates may have done little to attract new firms to the region, they have permitted indigenous manufacturing firms to be profitable. The fact that the bulk of New England's population has gradually moved to the better-situated metropolitan areas in southern New England has tended to keep regional wage levels reasonably close to the national average.

The increasing manufacturing specialization in technical and labor-intensive products has also helped the recent development of the New England economy. In his famous 1953 study,[2] Professor Leontief showed that the United States exports labor-intensive products and imports capital-intensive and resource-intensive products. This was a surprising finding, because this country has the highest wage rates in the world and what appears to be a very generous supply of natural resources and capital. The question naturally arises: Why should the United States be exporting manufactured products which require large amounts of labor—the scarce factor of production?

The logical explanation appears to be that no other country in the world has the technological capability of the industry and work force in the United States.[3] As a result, the nation exports items such as jet aircraft, specialized manufacturing equipment and machinery, industrial instrumentation, scientific laboratory equipment, and advanced medical equipment. These products are labor-intensive and are manufactured with a knowledgeable, well-trained labor force. These are also the types of products which can be manufactured in New England and then sold at competitive prices in national and world markets. It appears, therefore, that the future of New England's economy rests with the new technologically oriented manufacturing and service industries rather than with old-line industries such as textiles, shoes and leather, and apparel. So far as public policy is concerned, this suggests that the New England states should place increasing emphasis on providing high-quality secondary-school and college training so as to provide the necessary high-skilled labor force for the region's growing industries.

Labor-intensive specialization in New England manufacturing differs from that in many foreign countries and on many farms in the United States. In southeastern United States, for example, much of the farm population is redundant. It is only a very inefficient substitute for a small amount of fertilizer or a small amount of capital equipment. In New England, on the other hand, the work force generally uses the same tools, equipment, and techniques found elsewhere in the country. Here, the nature of the products requires labor-intensive production techniques. It is doubtful that the productivity of New England's population and public and private capital would be greatly increased even if they were, somehow, relocated in the Midwest. New England's locational disadvantages are not significant for the types of production which now predominate in the region.

Samuelson[4] has shown that under certain circumstances a poorly endowed country might enjoy living standards which are as high as those prevailing in a nation well endowed with natural resources. The circumstances he has postulated are free commodity trade (but not free movement of the factors of production), negligible transportation costs between the countries, the availability of the same production techniques in both countries, and only partial specialization in labor-intensive production or resource-intensive production in each of the countries.

These circumstances largely fit the relationship between New England and the rest of the United States. Transportation costs are significant between New England and other parts of the country, but otherwise, Samuelson's poorly endowed country is a reasonably good model of the New England economy. Manufacturing in the region is labor-intensive, and the same type of technology is used here as in the rest of the nation. The population thus enjoys a standard of living which is very similar to that in other parts of the country. Without trade with the other states, however, income levels in the New England states would be very low indeed.

It is interesting to speculate what would happen if every member of the labor force suddenly became very mobile and could easily be induced to move long distances for minor improvements in wage rates. Undoubtedly, the nation's Gross National Product would increase at a slightly faster rate during the adjustment period. At the same time, the population of many parts of New England, the South, and the Lake states would likely decline. It is probable that the population growth rate of the best located metropolitan areas in the Midwest, the Middle Atlantic states, and the Far West would rapidly accelerate.

Such population movements would help raise the level of wages in the nation's pockets of poverty. However, it would also change the distribution of population and the American landscape. Some regions would decline, and many small-town and rural areas would lose most of their population. Although greater labor mobility would bring substantial economic changes, its social and political consequences would be even more significant.

NOTES

Chapter II: NEW ENGLAND'S COMPETITIVE POSITION

1. R. A. Easterlin, "Interregional Differences in Per Capita Income, Population and Total Income, U.S., 1840–1950," National Bureau of Economic Research, *Conference on Research in Income and Wealth,* September 4–5, 1957 (mimeo.), as cited by Harvey S. Perloff *et al., Regions, Resources, and Economic Growth* (Baltimore: Johns Hopkins Press, 1960), p. 113.

2. Perloff, *op. cit.,* p. 120.

3. Romney Robinson, "Water Transportation and New England: An Economic Survey of the New England Seaports" (A Report to the New England Governors' Committee on Public Transportation), *Public Transportation for New England, Report No. 8* (Boston: The Committee, 1957), pp. 34–35.

4. Edgar M. Hoover, *Location Theory and the Shoe and Leather Industries* (Cambridge, Mass.: Harvard University Press, 1937), pp. 218–219.

5. Perloff, *op. cit.,* p. 112 (note).

6. Stuart U. Rich, "Product Policies of Nonintegrated New England Paper Companies" (unpublished Doctor of Business Administration dissertation, Graduate School of Business Administration, Harvard University, 1960), p. 23.

7. Lance Edwin Davis, "Stock Ownership in the Early New England Textile Industry," *The Business History Review,* XXXII (Summer, 1958), 204–210.

8. William H. Miernyk, "Labor Cost and Labor Supply as Determinants of Industrial Location" (unpublished Ph.D. dissertation, Department of Economics, Harvard University, 1953), pp. 109–112.

9. Committee on the New England Economy of the U.S. Council of Economic Advisers, *The New England Economy: A Report to the President . . .* (Washington, D.C.: U.S. Government Printing Office, 1951).

Penelope C. Hartland, *Balance of Interregional Payments of New England* (Brown University Studies, Vol. XIV) (Providence, R.I.: Brown University, 1950).

Seymour E. Harris, *The Economics of New England* (Cambridge, Mass.: Harvard University Press, 1952).

Committee of New England of the National Planning Association, *The Economic State of New England* (New Haven: Yale University Press, 1954).

New England Governors' Committee on Public Transportation, *Public Transportation for New England* (A series of ten reports to the New England Governors' Conference) (Boston: The Committee, 1957).

New England–New York Inter-Agency Committee, *The Resources of the New England–New York Region* (Part I. *The General Report;* Part II. *The*

Technical Report, in 39 chapters; Part III. *Reference Data,* in 3 volumes) (New York: The Committee, 1955).

[Arthur A. Bright, Jr.], "Industrial Power Costs in New England," *Monthly Review: Federal Reserve Bank of Boston,* XXXII (June, 1950), 1–13.

[Robert W. Eisenmenger], "Industrial Fuel Costs in New England," *New England Business Review: Federal Reserve Bank of Boston,* August, 1957, pp. 1–4; October, 1957, pp. 5–7.

William D. Shipman, *An Inquiry into the High Cost of Electricity in New England* (Middletown, Conn.: Wesleyan University Press, 1962).

John Donald Black, *The Rural Economy of New England* (Cambridge, Mass.: Harvard University Press, 1950).

R. C. Estall, *New England, A Study in Industrial Adjustment* (London: G. Bell and Sons, Ltd., 1966; New York: Frederick A. Praeger, 1966).

10. Robert W. Eisenmenger, *Fuel and Energy Use in the 1960's* (Research Report to the Federal Reserve Bank of Boston: 1970 Projection No. 9) (Boston: Federal Reserve Bank of Boston, 1959), pp. 21–25.

[Michael Rieber], "Crude Oil Import Restrictions," *New England Business Review: Federal Reserve Bank of Boston,* November, 1961, pp. 1–4.

11. Eisenmenger, *Fuel and Energy Use in the 1960's,* p. 6.

12. Michael Rieber, *Residual Oil Import Restrictions* (Research Report to the Federal Reserve Bank of Boston, No. 16) (Boston: Federal Reserve Bank of Boston, 1961), pp. 11, 11a.

13. H. B. Shepard, *Hardwood Pulp: Its Manufacture and Use* (Boston: The New England Council, 1956), p. 46.

14. William H. Miernyk and Arthur A. Bright, Jr., *The Textile Industries of New England* (Staff Memorandum No. 10 of the Committee of New England of the National Planning Association) (Boston: Federal Reserve Bank of Boston, 1952), pp. 25–27.

15. Shipman, *op. cit.,* p. 64.

16. Committee of New England of the National Planning Association, *op. cit.,* pp. 203–207.

17. Robert W. Eisenmenger, "Holyoke Water Power Company vs. Municipal Gas and Electric Department" (unpublished honors thesis, Department of Economics, Amherst College, 1949), pp. 9–13, 20–21.

18. Harris, *op. cit.,* Chapter 21, "Fuel, Power, and River Development," pp. 225–239.

19. Bright, *op. cit.,* pp. 12–13.

20. William H. Hughes, "The Efficient Organization of the Privately Owned Electric Utility Industry in the United States" (unpublished Ph.D. dissertation, Department of Economics, Harvard University, 1959), pp. 273–274.

21. Shipman, *op. cit.,* pp. 190–198.

22. John M. Wilkinson, "New England Power Developments: Part I. . . . the private utility industry," *New England Business Review: Federal Reserve Bank of Boston,* February, 1966, p. 17.

23. Helen H. Lamale and Margaret S. Stotz, "The Interim City Worker's Family Budget," *Monthly Labor Review,* LXXXIII (August, 1960), 788.

Margaret S. Stotz, "The BLS Interim Budget for a Retired Couple," *Monthly Labor Review,* LXXXIII (November, 1960), 1146.

24. Interview with Joseph Conaty, Regional Price Economist, New England Regional Office of the U.S. Bureau of Labor Statistics, Boston, Mass., December 15, 1962.

25. Most of the material on railroad rates in this section was drawn from Chapter 12 of the Committee of New England of the National Planning Association publication *The Economic State of New England,* pp. 444–458. This chapter was written by William H. Miernyk.

26. Martin L. Lindahl, *Railroad Freight Rates and New England's Competitive Position* (A Research Report to accompany Report No. 9 of the New England Governors' Committee on Public Transportation, *Public Transportation for New England*) (Boston: The Committee, 1957).

27. U.S. Bureau of the Census, "Governmental Finances in 1963," *Governmental Finances in the United States* (Washington, D.C.: U.S. Bureau of the Census, November, 1964), Tables 16, 21, and 25.

28. John D. Strasma, *State and Local Taxation of Industry: Some Comparisons* (Research Report to the Federal Reserve Bank of Boston, No. 4) (Boston: Federal Reserve Bank of Boston, 1959).

29. U.S. Bureau of the Census, *Statistical Abstract of the United States: 1964* (Washington, D.C.: U.S. Government Printing Office, 1964), Table 163, p. 124.

30. Black, *op. cit.,* p. 180 and following.

31. U.S. Forest Service, *Timber Trends in the United States* (Forest Resource Report No. 17) (Washington, D.C.: U.S. Government Printing Office, February, 1965), Appendix 1, Table 1, pp. 140–141.

32. U.S. Bureau of Mines, *Minerals Yearbook 1963.* Vol. 3. *Area Reports: Domestic* (Washington, D.C.: U.S. Government Printing Office, 1964), Table 4, p. 8.

33. U.S. Forest Service, *Timber Resources for America's Future* (Forest Resource Report No. 14) (Washington, D.C.: U.S. Government Printing Office, January, 1958), Appendix, Table 23, p. 550.

34. Solon L. Barraclough, "Forest Land Ownership in New England" (unpublished Ph.D. dissertation, Department of Economics, Harvard University, 1949).

35. U.S. Bureau of the Census, *U.S. Census of Manufactures: 1954.* Vol. I. *Summary Statistics* (Washington, D.C.: U.S. Government Printing Office, 1957), Table 2A, p. 210–21.

36. E. H. Boeckh & Associates, Inc., "Cost Indexes for 10 Types of Buildings," *Engineering News-Record,* March 18, 1965, p. 90.

37. "ENR Costs Report and Outlook," *Engineering News-Record,* December 20, 1962, pp. 87–89.

38. Robert L. Raimon, "Interstate Migration and Wage Theory," *The Review of Economics and Statistics,* XLIV (November, 1962), 431.

39. William Glenn Cunningham, *The Aircraft Industry: A Study in Industrial Location* (Los Angeles: L. L. Morrison, 1951), pp. 28–30, 169–170.

40. For a precise description of New England's climate see Black, *op. cit.,* pp. 35–44.

41. Committee of New England of the National Planning Association, *op. cit.,* p. 59.

42. Perloff, *op. cit.,* Appendix Table A–1, pp. 622–623, and Appendix Table A–5, pp. 630–631.

43. U.S. Fish and Wildlife Service, *Fishery Statistics of the United States: 1950* (Washington, D.C: U.S. Government Printing Office, 1953), pp. 59, 67.

U.S. Fish and Wildlife Service, *Fishery Statistics of the United States: 1963* (Washington, D.C.: U.S. Government Printing Office, 1965), pp. 94, 103.

U.S. Bureau of the Census, *Census of Manufactures: 1963* (Preliminary Reports Series MC63[P] 20C–1 and 20C–6) (Washington, D.C.: U.S. Government Printing Office, 1965).

44. Frederick W. Bell, *The Economics of the New England Fishing Industry: The Role of Technological Change and Government Aid* (Research Report to the Federal Reserve Bank of Boston, No. 31) (Boston: Federal Reserve Bank of Boston, 1966), Chapter VIII.

45. U.S. Fish and Wildlife Service, *loc. cit.*

U.S. Bureau of the Census, *Census of Manufactures: 1963.*

46. Robinson, *op. cit.,* p. 16.

47. *Ibid.,* p. 35.

48. Howard L. Green, "The Reach of New York City and Boston into Southern New England" (unpublished Ph.D. dissertation, Division of Geological Sciences, Harvard University, 1952), pp. 82–86.

David J. Ashton, *New England Manufacturers' Export Practice and Potential* (Research Report to the Federal Reserve Bank of Boston, No. 9) (Boston: Federal Reserve Bank of Boston, 1960), pp. 42–51.

49. U.S. Army. Corps of Engineers, *Waterborne Commerce of the United States: Calendar Year 1963.* Part I. *Waterways and Harbors—Atlantic Coast* (New York: U.S. Army. Corps of Engineers, North Atlantic Division [1964]), pp. 13–14, 131–133.

50. Robinson, *op. cit.,* p. 26.

51. U.S. Army. Corps of Engineers, *op. cit.,* pp. 13–15.

Chapter III: WAGES, SALARIES, AND INCOME IN NEW ENGLAND

1. Most studies of fringe benefits have shown that employees in high-wage industries receive proportionately more fringe benefits than employees in low-wage industries. The available evidence suggests that this is true in each region. See:

Lloyd G. Reynolds, *The Structure of Labor Markets* (New York: Harper, 1951), pp. 202–203.

Chamber of Commerce of the United States, *Fringe Benefits 1963* (Research Study prepared by the Economic Research Department) (Washington, D.C.: The Chamber, 1964), pp. 10, 15.

Scott E. Pardee, "A Study of Inter-City Wage Differentials" (unpublished Ph.D. dissertation, Department of Economics and Social Science, Massachusetts Institute of Technology, 1962), p. 29.

2. "New England Manufacturing. . . . Its Future Prospects," *Monthly Review: Federal Reserve Bank of Boston,* XXXI (September, 1949), 1–11.

3. Committee of New England of the National Planning Association, *The Economic State of New England* (New Haven: Yale University Press, 1954), p. 355.

4. William H. Miernyk and Arthur A. Bright, Jr., *The Textile Industries of New England* (Staff Memorandum No. 10 of the Committee of New England of the National Planning Association) (Boston: Federal Reserve Bank of Boston, 1952), p. 34.

5. Richard A. Lester, "Effectiveness of Factory Labor: South–North Comparisons," *Journal of Political Economy,* LIV (February, 1946), 60–75.

6. Martin Segal, *Wages in the Metropolis: Their Influence on the Location of Industries in the New York Region* (Cambridge, Mass.: Harvard University Press, 1960), pp. 27–34.

7. *Ibid.,* pp. 30, 31, 34.

8. Ronald C. Buehner, "The Effect of Walsh-Healey Minimum Wages on Regional Industries" (unpublished Master's thesis, School of Industrial Management, Massachusetts Institute of Technology, 1962), Appendix B.

9. Lloyd G. Reynolds and Cynthia H. Taft, *The Evolution of Wage Structure* (New Haven: Yale University Press, 1956), pp. 180–182.

10. U.S. Bureau of Labor Statistics, *Wages and Related Benefits.* Part I. *80 Metropolitan Areas, 1963–64* (Bulletin No. 1385–82) (Washington, D.C.: U.S. Government Printing Office, 1964).

————, *Industry Wage Survey: Machinery Manufacturing, March–May 1964* (Bulletin No. 1429) (Washington, D.C.: U.S. Government Printing Office, 1965).

11. Pardee, *op. cit.*

12. Edwin F. Estle, "Electronics on the Move," *New England Business Review: Federal Reserve Bank of Boston,* January, 1966, pp. 11–15.

13. Marguerite I. Coughlin, *Outlook for New England's Shoe Industry to 1970* (Research Report to the Federal Reserve Bank of Boston: 1970 Projection No. 14) (Boston: Federal Reserve Bank of Boston, 1959), pp. 8–9.

14. For a description of the sources used in this section, see Appendix B.

15. Clarence D. Long, *The Labor Force under Changing Income and Employment* (A Study by the National Bureau of Economic Research, No. 65, General Series) (Princeton, N.J.: Princeton University Press, 1958), pp. 82–88.

16. This situation existed in 1960. Throughout most of the post–World War II period, unemployment was higher in New England than in the United States. See Chapter V.

Chapter IV: WAGE THEORY

1. Joseph W. Bloch, "Regional Wage Differentials: 1907–46," *Monthly Labor Review,* LXVI (April, 1948), 371–377.

2. Martin Segal, "Regional Wage Differences in Manufacturing in the Postwar Period," *The Review of Economics and Statistics,* XLIII (May, 1961), 148–155.

3. Carter Goodrich *et al., Migration and Economic Opportunity: The Report of the Study of Population Redistribution* (Philadelphia: University of Pennsylvania Press, 1936), Chapter II, esp. pp. 54–67, 73–74.

4. Lloyd G. Reynolds, *The Structure of Labor Markets* (New York: Harper, 1951), pp. 77–79.

5. William H. Miernyk, *Inter-Industry Labor Mobility: The Case of the Displaced Textile Worker* (Boston: Northeastern University, Bureau of Business and Economic Research, 1955), pp. 26–28.

6. Martin Segal, *Wages in the Metropolis* (Cambridge, Mass.: Harvard University Press, 1960), pp. 95–96.

7. Larry A. Sjaastad, "Income and Migration in the United States" (unpublished Ph.D. dissertation, Department of Economics, University of Chicago, 1961), p. 71.

8. James S. Duesenberry, *Business Cycles and Economic Growth* (New York: McGraw-Hill, 1958), pp. 299–309.

9. This description of the industrial-composition theory of interarea wage differentials has been spliced together from the separate ideas of numerous researchers who are mentioned in the following pages.

10. Richard Ruggles, "The Nature of Price Flexibility and the Determinants of Relative Price Changes in the Economy," National Bureau of Economic Research, *Business Concentration and Price Policy* (A Conference of the Universities–National Bureau Committee for Economic Research) (Princeton, N.J.: Princeton University Press, 1955), pp. 441–495.

11. Sumner H. Slichter, "Notes on the Structure of Wages," *The Review of Economics and Statistics,* XXXII (February, 1950), 80–91.

12. Reynolds, *op. cit.,* p. 232.

13. John T. Dunlop, "Productivity and Wage Structure," in L. A. Metzler *et al., Income, Employment, and Public Policy: Essays in Honor of Alvin H. Hansen* (New York: Norton, 1948), pp. 341–362.

14. Joseph W. Garbarino, "A Theory of Interindustry Wage Structure," *The Quarterly Journal of Economics,* LXIV (May, 1950), 300–302.

15. Richard A. Lester, "Wage Diversity and Its Theoretical Implications," *The Review of Economics and Statistics,* XXVIII (August, 1946), 152–159.

16. Reynolds, *op. cit.,* pp. 184–189.

17. International Economic Association, *The Theory of Wage Determination* (Proceedings of a Conference held by the International Economic Association, ed. John T. Dunlop) (New York: St. Martin's Press, 1957), pp. 3–22.

18. [Richard A. Walker], "Is There A 'Prevailing Wage'?" *New England Business Review: Federal Reserve Bank of Boston,* December, 1961, pp. 1–4.

19. Pittsburgh Regional Planning Association, *Region in Transition* (Pittsburgh, Penna.: University of Pittsburgh Press, 1963), pp. 75–111.

20. Stephen P. Sobotka, "Michigan's Employment Problem: The Substitution Against Labor," *The Journal of Business,* XXXIV (April, 1961), 119–128.

21. Otto Eckstein and Thomas A. Wilson, "Determination of Money Wages in American Industry," *The Quarterly Journal of Economics,* LXXVI (August, 1962), 379–414.

22. For example, in Chapter 4 of *Wages in the Metropolis,* Segal con-

cludes that sluggish migration helps maintain interarea wage differentials. He also shows, however, that some industries pay relatively high wages in all locations.

23. Scott E. Pardee, "A Study of Inter-City Wage Differentials" (unpublished Ph.D. dissertation, Department of Economics and Social Science, Massachusetts Institute of Technology, 1962), pp. 92–119.

24. *Ibid.,* p. 111.

25. *Ibid.,* p. 119.

26. Frank A. Hanna, *State Income Differentials 1919–1954* (Durham, N.C.: Duke University Press, 1959), p. 192.

27. *Ibid.,* p. 141.

28. Edward F. Denison, "Comment," in National Bureau of Economic Research, *Regional Income. Studies in Income and Wealth* (Volume 21 by the Conference on Research on Income and Wealth) (Princeton, N. J.: Princeton University Press, 1957), pp. 161–179.

29. Pardee, *op. cit.,* p. 94.

Chapter V: UNEMPLOYMENT, MIGRATION, AND MANUFACTURING WAGE RATES IN NEW ENGLAND

1. William H. Miernyk, *New England Textile Employment in 1970* (Research Report to the Federal Reserve Bank of Boston: 1970 Projection No. 16) (Boston: Federal Reserve Bank of Boston, 1959).

2. For a discussion of recent trends in wage rates in New England resulting from low unemployment rates, see Edwin F. Estle, "New England's Wage Level Approaches National Average," *New England Business Review: Federal Reserve Bank of Boston,* March, 1966, pp. 2–7.

Chapter VI: MANUFACTURING SPECIALIZATION IN NEW ENGLAND

1. Stuart U. Rich, "Product Policies of Nonintegrated New England Paper Companies" (unpublished Doctor of Business Administration dissertation, Graduate School of Business Administration, Harvard University, 1960), pp. 393–436.

"Achieving Success in Specialty Paper," *New England Business Review: Federal Reserve Bank of Boston,* September, 1960, pp. 1–4.

Helen M. Hunter, "United States International Trade in Wood Pulp: A Case Study in International Trade" (unpublished Ph.D. dissertation, Department of Economics, Harvard University, 1952), pp. 132–150.

2. Kenneth Paul Wickman, "Historical and Locational Aspects of Economic Decline in the New England Furniture Industry" (unpublished Ph.D. dissertation, Department of Economics, Syracuse University, 1962), pp. 139, 362–363.

3. "Textile Trends," *New England Business Review: Federal Reserve Bank of Boston,* December, 1960, pp. 5–7.

Interview with Daniel Gordon of the Northern Textile Association, Boston, Mass., March 14, 1963.

4.   George H. Ellis, "Postwar Industrial Location in New England" (unpublished Ph.D. dissertation, Department of Economics, Harvard University, 1949), pp. 170–171.

5.   Albert H. Rubenstein and Victor L. Andrews, *The Electronics Industry in New England to 1970* (Research Report to the Federal Reserve Bank of Boston: 1970 Projection No. 4) (Boston: Federal Reserve Bank of Boston, 1959), pp. 5–11.

Raphael W. Hodgson, *Interview Reports on the Effects of Trade Liberalization on New England Manufacturing* (Research Report to the Federal Reserve Bank of Boston, No. 22) (Boston: Federal Reserve Bank of Boston, 1963), pp. 1–11, 31–56.

6.   Harvey S. Perloff *et al., Regions, Resources, and Economic Growth* (Baltimore: Johns Hopkins Press, 1960), pp. 572–574.

7.   Paul S. Anderson, "The Apparent Decline in Capital-Output Ratios," *The Quarterly Journal of Economics,* LXXV (November, 1961), 615–634.

8.   This was the theory implicit in an article written by Dr. T. Y. Shen. See "Investment and Productivity in New England Manufacturing Industries: Part 1, The Background," *New England Business Review: Federal Reserve Bank of Boston,* January, 1960, pp. 7–9.

For related discussions of the same topic see:

C. E. Ferguson, "Cross-Section Production Functions and the Elasticity of Substitution in American Manufacturing Industry," *The Review of Economics and Statistics,* XLV (August, 1963), 305–313.

Matityahu Marcus, "Capital-Labor Substitution Among States: Some Empirical Evidence," *The Review of Economics and Statistics,* XLVI (November, 1964), 434–438.

Frederick W. Bell, "A Note on the Empirical Estimation of the CES Production Function with the Use of Capital Data," *The Review of Economics and Statistics,* XLVII (August, 1965), 328–330.

9.   Victor R. Fuchs, *Changes in the Location of Manufacturing in the United States Since 1929* (New Haven: Yale University Press, 1962), p. 167.

Chapter VII: ADVANTAGES OF THE HEAD START

1.   George H. Ellis, "Postwar Industrial Location in New England" (unpublished Ph.D. dissertation, Department of Economics, Harvard University, 1949), pp. 159–209, 258–268.

2.   Kenneth Paul Wickman, "Historical and Locational Aspects of Economic Decline in the New England Furniture Industry" (unpublished Ph.D. dissertation, Department of Economics, Syracuse University, 1962), pp. 141–183.

3.   Ellis, *op. cit.,* p. 198.

4.   Wickman, *op. cit.,* pp. 145–154, 232–390.

5.   Helen M. Hunter, "Innovation, Competition, and Locational Changes in the Pulp and Paper Industry: 1880–1950," *Land Economics,* XXXI (November, 1955), 314–327.

6.   William H. Miernyk, "Labor Cost and Labor Supply as Determinants of Industrial Location" (unpublished Ph.D. dissertation, Department of Economics, Harvard University, 1953), pp. 158–162.

7. *Ibid.*, pp. 270–273.

8. *Ibid.*, pp. 409–412.

9. George Katona and James N. Morgan, "The Quantitative Study of Factors Determining Business Decisions," *The Quarterly Journal of Economics*, LXVI (February, 1952), 67–82.

10. Melvin L. Greenhut, *Plant Location in Theory and in Practise: The Economics of Space* (Chapel Hill, N.C.: University of North Carolina Press, 1956, pp. 276–277.

11. Colin Clark, *The Conditions of Economic Progress* (London: Macmillan, 1940), p. 182.

12. Harvey S. Perloff *et al.*, *Regions, Resources, and Economic Growth* (Baltimore: Johns Hopkins Press, 1960), Appendix Table C, pp. 642–645.

13. Penelope C. Hartland, *Balance of Interregional Payments of New England* (Providence, R.I.: Brown University, 1950), pp. 101–105.

14. Paul Hendrick, Richard L. Pfister, and Martin Segal, *Vacation Travel Business in New Hampshire: A Survey and Analysis* (Concord, N.H.: New Hampshire Department of Resources and Economic Development, 1962), pp. 65–88.

Arnold H. Raphaelson, Tadeusz A. Siedlik, and John D. Coupe, *A Study of the Vacation Industry in Maine* (Orono, Maine: University of Maine, School of Business Administration, 1961), pp. 103–111.

15. Francis S. Doody, *The Immediate Economic Impact of Higher Education in New England* (Education Studies, New Series, No. 1) (Boston: Boston University, Bureau of Business Research, 1961).

16. Frederick W. Bell, "Changing Specialization and Bay State Growth," *New England Business Review: Federal Reserve Bank of Boston*, April, 1965, pp. 2–8.

17. Federal Reserve Bank of Boston, *Annual Report, 1961: New England at Work in the Space Age* (Boston: Federal Reserve Bank of Boston, 1962), p. 9.

18. Simon Kuznets, Ann Ratner Miller, and Richard A. Easterlin, *Population Redistribution and Economic Growth: United States, 1870–1950.* Vol. II. *Analyses of Economic Change* (Philadelphia: The American Philosophical Society, 1960), p. 114.

Chapter VIII: CONCLUSIONS AND IMPLICATIONS

1. Larry A. Sjaastad, "Income and Migration in the United States" (unpublished Ph.D. dissertation, Department of Economics, University of Chicago, 1961), p. 71.

2. Wassily Leontief, "Domestic Production and Foreign Trade; The American Capital Position Re-examined," in *Proceedings of the American Philosophical Society*, September 28, 1953 (reprinted in *Economia Internazionale*, Genoa, 1954, No. 1).

3. Donald B. Keesing, "Labor Skills and International Trade: Evaluating Many Trade Flows with a Single Measuring Device," *The Review of Economics and Statistics*, LXVII (August, 1965), 287–294.

4. Paul A. Samuelson, "International Trade and Equalization of Factor Prices," *Economic Journal*, LVIII (June, 1948), 163–184.

APPENDIX A

TABLE A–1

Metropolitan Areas outside New England Used in
Wage Comparisons with Boston, Providence, and Worcester:
Plant and Office Occupations in Manufacturing
(Tables A–2—A–4)
1951–1952, 1960–1961, and 1963–1964

Middle Atlantic	*Middle West*
Albany–Schenectady–Troy	Chicago
Allentown–Bethlehem–Easton	Cincinnati
Buffalo	Cleveland
Newark–Jersey City	Columbus
New York	Detroit
Philadelphia	Indianapolis
Pittsburgh	Kansas City
Scranton	Louisville
Trenton	Milwaukee
	Minneapolis–St. Paul
	St. Louis

South	*Far West*
Atlanta	Denver
Birmingham	Los Angeles
Houston	Phoenix
Jacksonville	Salt Lake City
Memphis	San Francisco–Oakland
New Orleans	Seattle
Norfolk–Portsmouth	
Oklahoma City	
Richmond	

SOURCE: U.S. Bureau of Labor Statistics, *Wages and Related Benefits: 40 Labor Markets, 1951–1952* (Bulletin No. 1113) (Washington, D.C.: U.S. Government Printing Office, [1952]).

125

TABLE A-2

Average Straight-Time Hourly Earnings of Men in 15 Plant Occupations in Manufacturing (Maintenance and Power Plant) in Areas outside New England and in Boston, Providence, and Worcester, 1951–1952, 1960–1961, and 1963–1964

Occupation (in order of ascending average earnings in 1963–1964)	Areas outside New England				Boston			Providence			Worcester		
	Number in Average	Average[a]											
		1951–1952	1960–1961	1963–1964	1951–1952	1960–1961	1963–1964	1951–1952	1960–1961	1963–1964	1951–1952	1960–1961	1963–1964
Trades helpers	29	$1.52	$2.30	$2.47	$1.54	$2.18	$2.46	$1.38	$1.99	$2.18	$1.51	$1.97	$2.14
Oilers	28	1.53	2.38	2.63	1.43	2.23	2.34	1.35	1.73	1.90	1.47	2.28	2.51
Stationary boiler firemen	27	1.54	2.40	2.65	1.59	2.35	2.54	1.40	1.90	2.09	1.49	2.28	2.34
Automotive mechanics	31	1.79	2.70	2.96	1.84	2.58	2.89	1.54	n.a.	2.59	1.53	2.63	2.77
Mechanics	31	1.83	2.79	3.04	1.75	2.55	2.75	1.66	2.29	2.55	1.76	2.68	2.81
Carpenters	28	1.86	2.83	3.07	1.79	2.61	2.85	1.65	2.19	2.36	1.67	2.45	2.53
Painters	27	1.84	2.84	3.11	1.73	2.57	2.90	1.49	2.19	2.36	1.61	2.54	n.a.
Stationary engineers	26	1.92	2.93	3.21	1.92	2.83	3.01	1.78	2.28	2.43	1.75	2.64	2.94
Electricians	31	1.94	2.98	3.25	1.92	2.83	3.06	1.65	2.35	2.62	1.79	2.83	3.01
Machine-tool operators, toolroom	16	1.95	2.98	3.26	n.a.	2.63	2.96	n.a.	2.34	2.58	1.77	2.39	2.65
Pipefitters	23	1.97	3.00	3.26	1.86	2.78	3.04	1.65	2.34	2.59	1.77	2.76	2.93
Machinists	29	1.96	3.00	3.27	1.88	2.85	3.01	1.65	2.42	2.68	1.85	2.79	2.86
Millwrights	23	1.93	3.02	3.27	1.78	2.66	2.91	1.66	2.32	2.65	1.77	2.59	2.68
Sheet-metal workers	17	1.99	3.06	3.35	1.84	2.73	3.02	1.72	2.49	n.a.	n.a.	n.a.	2.86
Tool and die makers	24	2.12	3.16	3.42	2.02	3.02	3.23	1.79	2.84	3.17	1.82	2.67	2.82

[a] Average of hourly earnings for each occupation based on areas for which data are available in all three time periods.

SOURCES: U.S. Bureau of Labor Statistics, *Wages and Related Benefits: 40 Labor Markets, 1951–1952* (Bulletin No. 1113) (Washington, D.C.: U.S. Government Printing Office, [1952]), Table A-2a.

———, *Wages and Related Benefits: 82 Labor Markets, 1960–1961* (Bulletin No. 1285–83) (Washington, D.C.: U.S. Government Printing Office, 1961), Table A-10.

TABLE A–2a

Average Hourly Earnings for 15 Plant Occupations in Manufacturing (Maintenance and Power Plant) in Boston, Providence, and Worcester Relative to Average Earnings in Areas outside New England, 1951–1952, 1960–1961, and 1963–1964

For each occupation and time period, average of hourly earnings in areas outside New England shown in Table A–2 = 100

Occupation (in order of ascending average of earnings in 1963–1964)	Number of Areas in Average	Boston			Providence			Worcester		
		1951–1952	1960–1961	1963–1964	1951–1952	1960–1961	1963–1964	1951–1952	1960–1961	1963–1964
Trades helpers	29	101.3	94.8	99.6	90.8	86.5	88.3	99.3	85.7	86.6
Oilers	28	93.5	93.7	89.0	88.2	72.7	72.2	96.1	95.8	95.4
Stationary boiler firemen	27	103.2	97.9	95.8	90.9	79.2	78.9	96.8	95.0	88.3
Automotive mechanics	31	102.8	95.6	97.6	86.0	n.a.	87.5	85.5	97.4	93.6
Mechanics	31	95.6	91.4	90.5	90.7	82.1	83.9	96.2	96.1	92.4
Carpenters	28	96.2	92.2	92.8	88.7	77.4	76.9	89.8	86.6	82.4
Painters	27	94.0	90.5	93.2	81.0	77.1	75.9	87.5	89.4	n.a.
Stationary engineers	26	100.0	96.6	93.8	92.7	77.8	75.7	91.1	90.1	91.6
Electricians	31	99.0	95.0	94.2	85.0	78.9	80.6	92.3	95.0	92.6

TABLE A–2a *(continued)*

Occupation (in order of ascending average of earnings in 1963–1964)	Number of Areas in Average	Boston			Providence			Worcester		
		1951–1952	1960–1961	1963–1964	1951–1952	1960–1961	1963–1964	1951–1952	1960–1961	1963–1964
Machine-tool operators, toolroom	16	n.a.	88.3	90.8	n.a.	78.5	79.1	90.8	80.2	81.3
Pipefitters	23	94.4	92.7	93.3	83.8	78.0	79.4	89.8	92.0	90.0
Machinists	29	95.9	95.0	92.0	84.2	80.7	82.0	94.4	93.0	87.5
Millwrights	23	92.2	88.1	89.0	86.0	76.8	81.0	91.7	85.8	82.0
Sheet-metal workers	17	92.5	89.2	90.1	86.4	81.4	n.a.	n.a.	n.a.	85.4
Tool and die makers	24	95.3	95.6	94.4	84.4	89.9	92.7	85.8	84.5	82.5

SOURCE: See Table A–2.

TABLE A–2b

Distribution of Earnings Relatives for 15 Plant Occupations in Manufacturing (Maintenance and Power Plant): Occupations in Boston, Providence, and Worcester Classified According to Size of Earnings Relative to Earnings in Areas outside New England, 1951–1952, 1960–1961, and 1963–1964

Distribution of earnings relatives shown in Table A–2a

Size of Relative	Boston			Providence			Worcester		
	1951–52	1960–61	1963–64	1951–52	1960–61	1963–64	1951–52	1960–61	1963–64
105 and over	—	—	—	—	—	—	—	—	—
100–104	4	7	1	—	—	—	—	—	—
95–99	5	5	2	4	1	1	4	5	1
90–94	5	3	10	6	1	2	7	3	5
85–89	—	—	2	4	3	4	3	5	4
80–84	—	—	—	—	8	6	—	1	4
75–79	—	—	—	—	1	1	—	—	—
70–74	—	—	—	—	—	—	—	—	—
TOTAL NUMBER OF OCCUPATIONS	14	15	15	14	14	14	14	14	14

SOURCE: See Table A–2.

TABLE A-2c

Average Hourly Earnings for 15 Plant Occupations in Manufacturing (Maintenance and Power Plant): Lowest, Median, and Highest Earnings in Areas outside New England,[a] and Number of These Areas with Earnings Below or Equal[b] to Earnings in Boston, Providence, and Worcester, 1951–1952, 1960–1961, and 1963–1964

| Occupation (in order of ascending average earnings in 1963–1964) | No. of Areas in Group | Areas outside New England Average Hourly Earnings Lowest, Median, Highest | | | Number of Areas outside New England with Average Hourly Earnings Below or Equal to Earnings in | | | | | | | | |
| | | | | | BOSTON | | | PROVIDENCE | | | WORCESTER | | |
		1951–1952	1960–1961	1963–1964	1951–1952	1960–1961	1963–1964	1951–1952	1960–1961	1963–1964	1951–1952	1960–1961	1963–1964
Trades helpers	29	$1.10	$1.71	$1.83	14	8	14	5	4	2	11 (2)[b]	3	2
		1.56	2.29	2.53									
		1.84	2.69	2.85									
Oilers	28	1.11	1.91	2.14	5	6	3 (1)	3	0	0	6 (1)	7	7
		1.56	2.44	2.67									
		1.79	2.65	3.07									
Stationary boiler firemen	27	1.13	1.46	1.59	13	10	7	6	4	3	9	7 (1)	4
		1.62	2.48	2.67									
		1.91	2.99	3.32									
Automotive mechanics	31	1.42	2.05	2.28	17 (1)	9	9 (1)	4	n.a.	6	4	9	8
		1.83	2.78	3.03									
		2.16	3.29	3.69									
Mechanics	31	1.54	2.25	2.49	9	5	3	6	1	1	9	10	6
		1.85	2.79	3.07									
		2.16	3.28	3.54									

See footnotes at end of table.

TABLE A–2c (continued)

Occupation (in order of ascending average earnings in 1963-1964)	No. of Areas in Group	Areas outside New England — Average Hourly Earnings Lowest, Median, Highest			Number of Areas outside New England with Average Hourly Earnings Below or Equal to Earnings in								
					BOSTON			PROVIDENCE			WORCESTER		
		1951–1952	1960–1961	1963–1964	1951–1952	1960–1961	1963–1964	1951–1952	1960–1961	1963–1964	1951–1952	1960–1961	1963–1964
Carpenters	28	$1.50 / 1.87 / 2.14	$2.24 / 2.87 / 3.16	$2.30 / 3.11 / 3.47	6 (3)	3	2	3	0	1	3 (1)	2	1
Painters	27	1.53 / 1.86 / 2.11	2.44 / 2.83 / 3.22	2.62 / 3.09 / 3.53	6	2	2	0	0	0	2 (1)	1	n.a.
Stationary engineers	26	1.56 / 1.90 / 2.22	2.40 / 2.93 / 3.37	2.72 / 3.17 / 3.78	14 (1)	10	7 (1)	5	0	0	3	5 (1)	5 (1)
Electricians	31	1.66 / 1.94 / 2.16	2.55 / 3.01 / 3.33	2.73 / 3.25 / 3.64	13 (1)	5	4	0	0	0	4	5	3
Machine-tool operators, toolroom	16	1.57 / 1.95 / 2.22	2.61 / 3.00 / 3.30	2.85 / 3.30 / 3.57	n.a.	1	1	n.a.	0	0	1	0	0
Pipefitters	23	1.52 / 1.97 / 2.23	2.65 / 3.01 / 3.28	2.88 / 3.26 / 3.50	4	2	2	1	0	0	1	2	1

See footnotes at end of table.

TABLE A–2c (*continued*)

Occupation (in order of ascending average earnings in 1963–1964)	No. of Areas in Group	Areas outside New England			Number of Areas outside New England with Average Hourly Earnings Below or Equal to Earnings in								
		Average Hourly Earnings Lowest, Median, Highest			BOSTON			PROVIDENCE			WORCESTER		
		1951–1952	1960–1961	1963–1964	1951–1952	1960–1961	1963–1964	1951–1952	1960–1961	1963–1964	1951–1952	1960–1961	1963–1964
Machinists	29	$1.60	$2.47	$2.79	6 (3)	7 (1)	2	1	0	0	5 (1)	4	1
		1.97	3.04	3.29									
		2.18	3.31	3.57									
Millwrights	23	1.65	2.72	3.00	2	0	0	1	0	0	2	0	0
		1.95	3.02	3.29									
		2.10	3.36	3.47									
Sheet-metal workers	17	1.80	2.83	3.07	2	0	0	0	0	n.a.	n.a.	n.a.	0
		1.99	3.08	3.35									
		2.34	3.35	3.70									
Tool and die makers	24	1.87	2.76	3.02	4	3	3 (1)	0	2	3	0	0	0
		2.13	3.16	3.43									
		2.37	3.53	3.90									

a For each occupation, areas are those for which data are available in all three time periods.

b Figures in parentheses indicate number of areas with earnings equal to earnings in Boston, Providence, or Worcester. Other figures indicate number of areas with lower earnings.

SOURCE: See Table A–2.

TABLE A-3

Average Straight-Time Hourly Earnings (of men, except where indicated) in 15 Plant Occupations in Manufacturing (Custodial, Warehousing, and Shipping) in Areas outside New England and in Boston, Providence, and Worcester, 1951–1952, 1960–1961, and 1963–1964

| Occupation (in order of ascending average earnings in 1963–1964) | Areas outside New England | | | | BOSTON | | | PROVIDENCE | | | WORCESTER | | |
| | Number in Average | Average[a] | | | | | | | | | | | |
		1951–1952	1960–1961	1963–1964	1951–1952	1960–1961	1963–1964	1951–1952	1960–1961	1963–1964	1951–1952	1960–1961	1963–1964
Janitors, porters, and cleaners (women)	23	$1.13	$1.73	$1.88	$1.14	$1.66	$1.88	$1.05	$1.43	$1.63	$1.21	$1.66	$1.72
Watchmen	32	1.23	1.77	1.92	1.23	1.84	2.01	1.21	1.54	1.70	1.26	1.87	1.84
Janitors, porters, and cleaners	34	1.24	1.91	2.10	1.26	1.90	1.98	1.16	1.53	1.68	1.24	1.78	1.95
Laborers, material handling	34	1.34	2.02	2.22	1.38	1.94	2.06	1.28	1.67	1.76	1.31	1.72	2.16
Packers, shipping	25	1.39	2.03	2.24	1.37	1.84	2.14	1.20	1.66	1.82	1.45	2.16	2.31
Truck drivers, light (under 1½ tons)	22	1.47	2.15	2.33	1.74	2.43	2.47	1.26	1.52	1.67	1.44	1.90	2.05
Order fillers	28	1.40	2.12	2.34	1.47	2.10	2.17	1.21	1.59	1.94	1.18	2.05	2.18
Receiving clerks	28	1.52	2.26	2.48	1.46	2.10	2.23	1.40	1.80	1.91	1.40	2.14	2.30
Truckers, power (fork lift)	34	1.49	2.26	2.48	1.57	2.19	2.45	1.35	1.95	2.15	1.43	2.28	2.40

See footnotes at end of table.

TABLE A–3 *(continued)*

Occupation (in order of ascending average earnings in 1963–1964)	Areas outside New England				Boston			Providence			Worcester		
	Number in Average	Average[a]			1951– 1952	1960– 1961	1963– 1964	1951– 1952	1960– 1961	1963– 1964	1951– 1952	1960– 1961	1963– 1964
		1951– 1952	1960– 1961	1963– 1964									
Shipping and receiving clerks	26	$1.51	$2.32	$2.50	$1.42	$2.21	$2.26	$1.27	$1.91	$2.04	$1.36	$2.04	$2.04
Shipping clerks	28	1.56	2.34	2.55	1.50	2.25	2.36	1.47	1.88	1.95	1.41	2.21	2.32
Guards	23	1.51	2.36	2.56	1.46	2.12	2.27	1.22	1.85	2.01	1.45	2.13	2.21
Truck drivers, medium (1½–4 tons)	30	1.54	2.38	2.62	1.63	2.46	2.68	1.34	1.91	2.15	1.30	2.01	2.03
Truckers, power (other than fork lift)	19	1.56	2.45	2.62	1.61	2.23	2.48	1.32	1.80	2.09	1.53	2.42	2.66
Truck drivers, heavy (over 4 tons, trailer type)	18	1.64	2.56	2.76	1.69	2.44	2.64	1.42	2.15	2.32	1.44	n.a.	n.a.

[a] Average of hourly earnings for each occupation based on areas for which data are available in all three time periods.
SOURCES: U.S. Bureau of Labor Statistics, *Wages and Related Benefits: 40 Labor Markets, 1951–1952* (Bulletin No. 1113) (Washington, D.C.: U.S. Government Printing Office, [1952], Table A–2a.

———, *Wages and Related Benefits: 82 Labor Markets, 1960–61* (Bulletin No. 1285–83) (Washington, D.C.: U.S. Government Printing Office, 1961), Table A–10.

———, *Wages and Related Benefits. Part I. 80 Metropolitan Areas, 1963–64* (Bulletin No. 1385–82) (Washington, D.C.: U.S. Government Printing Office, 1964), Table A–10.

TABLE A-3a

Average Hourly Earnings for 15 Plant Occupations in Manufacturing (Custodial, Warehousing, and Shipping) in Boston, Providence, and Worcester Relative to Average Earnings in Areas outside New England, 1951–1952, 1960–1961, and 1963–1964

For each occupation and time period, average of hourly earnings in areas outside New England shown in Table A–3 = 100

Occupation (in order of ascending average earnings in 1963–1964)	Number of Areas in Average	Boston			Providence			Worcester		
		1951–1952	1960–1961	1963–1964	1951–1952	1960–1961	1963–1964	1951–1952	1960–1961	1963–1964
Janitors, porters, and cleaners (women)	23	100.9	96.0	100.0	92.9	82.7	86.7	107.1	96.0	91.5
Watchmen	32	100.0	104.0	104.7	98.4	87.0	88.5	102.4	105.6	95.8
Janitors, porters, and cleaners	34	101.6	99.5	94.3	93.5	80.1	80.0	100.0	93.2	92.9
Laborers, material handling	34	103.0	96.0	92.8	95.5	82.7	79.3	97.8	85.1	97.3
Packers, shipping	25	98.6	90.6	95.5	86.3	81.8	81.3	104.3	106.4	103.1
Truck drivers, light (under 1½ tons)	22	118.4	113.0	106.0	85.7	70.7	71.7	98.0	88.4	88.0
Order fillers	28	105.0	99.1	92.7	86.4	75.0	82.9	84.3	96.7	93.2

TABLE A–3a (continued)

Occupation (in order of ascending average earnings in 1963–1964)	Number of Areas in Average	BOSTON			PROVIDENCE			WORCESTER		
		1951–1952	1960–1961	1963–1964	1951–1952	1960–1961	1963–1964	1951–1952	1960–1961	1963–1964
Receiving clerks	28	96.1	92.9	89.9	92.1	79.6	77.0	92.1	94.7	92.7
Truckers, power (fork lift)	34	105.4	96.9	98.8	90.6	86.3	86.7	96.0	100.9	96.8
Shipping and receiving clerks	26	94.0	95.3	90.4	84.1	82.3	81.6	90.1	87.9	81.6
Shipping clerks	28	96.2	96.2	92.5	94.2	80.3	76.5	90.4	94.4	91.0
Guards	23	96.7	89.8	88.7	80.8	78.4	78.5	96.0	90.3	86.3
Truck drivers, medium (1½–4 tons)	30	105.8	103.4	102.3	87.0	80.3	82.1	84.4	84.5	77.5
Truckers, power (other than fork lift)	19	103.2	91.0	94.7	84.6	73.5	79.8	98.1	98.8	101.5
Truck drivers, heavy (over 4 tons, trailer type)	18	103.0	95.3	95.7	86.6	84.0	84.1	87.8	n.a.	n.a.

SOURCE: See Table A–3.

TABLE A-3b

Distribution of Earnings Relatives for 15 Plant Occupations in Manufacturing (Custodial, Warehousing, and Shipping): Occupations in Boston, Providence, and Worcester Classified According to Size of Earnings Relative to Earnings in Areas outside New England, 1951–1952, 1960–1961, and 1963–1964

Distribution of earnings relatives shown in Table A-3a.

Size of Relative	Boston			Providence			Worcester		
	1951–52	1960–61	1963–64	1951–52	1960–61	1963–64	1951–52	1960–61	1963–64
105 and over	4	1	2	—	—	—	1	2	—
100–104	6	3	2	—	—	—	3	1	2
95–99	4	7	4	2	—	—	5	4	3
90–94	1	4	6	5	—	—	3	3	5
85–89	—	—	1	6	2	3	1	4	2
80–84	—	—	—	2	9	7	2	—	1
75–79	—	—	—	—	2	4	—	—	1
70–74	—	—	—	—	2	1	—	—	—
TOTAL NUMBER OF OCCUPATIONS	15	15	15	15	15	15	15	14	14

SOURCE: See Table A-3.

TABLE A–3c

Average Hourly Earnings for 15 Plant Occupations in Manufacturing (Custodial, Warehousing, and Shipping): Lowest, Median, and Highest Earnings in Areas outside New England,[a] *and Number of These Areas with Earnings Below or Equal*[b] *to Earnings in Boston, Providence, and Worcester, 1951–1952, 1960–1961, and 1963–1964*

Occupation (in order of ascending average earnings in 1963–1964)	No. of Areas in Group	Average Hourly Earnings Lowest, Median, Highest 1951–1952	1960–1961	1963–1964	BOSTON 1951–1952	1960–1961	1963–1964	PROVIDENCE 1951–1952	1960–1961	1963–1964	WORCESTER 1951–1952	1960–1961	1963–1964
Janitors, porters, and cleaners (women)	23	$ .81	$1.27	$1.43	11 (1)	7	10 (1)	6 (1)	4	4	16	7	5
		1.14	1.74	1.91									
		1.52	2.06	2.21									
Watchmen	32	.88	1.14	1.27	13	18 (1)	19	12	6 (1)	9	18 (2)	20	12 (1)
		1.25	1.79	1.92									
		1.66	2.34	2.54									
Janitors, porters, and cleaners	34	.94	1.42	1.51	18	15	8	8	2 (1)	2	16 (1)	7	7
		1.25	1.96	2.13									
		1.60	2.38	2.58									
Laborers, material handling	34	.89	1.38	1.57	17	13	11	11	6	4 (1)	11 (1)	7	13
		1.37	2.10	2.30									
		1.70	2.48	2.78									
Packers, shipping	25	1.01	1.51	1.72	11	7	6 (2)	5	2	3	16	17	14
		1.39	2.08	2.27									
		1.75	2.43	2.66									

See footnotes at end of table.

TABLE A–3c (continued)

Occupation (in order of ascending average earnings in 1963–1964)	Areas outside New England — No. of Areas in Group	Average Hourly Earnings Lowest, Median, Highest 1951–1952	1960–1961	1963–1964	Number of Areas outside New England with Average Hourly Earnings Below or Equal to Earnings in — BOSTON 1951–1952	BOSTON 1960–1961	BOSTON 1963–1964	PROVIDENCE 1951–1952	PROVIDENCE 1960–1961	PROVIDENCE 1963–1964	WORCESTER 1951–1952	WORCESTER 1960–1961	WORCESTER 1963–1964
Truck drivers, light (under 1½ tons)	22	$.88	$1.40	$1.55	17 (1)	17	14	4 (1)	2	3	11 (1)	5	6
		1.43	2.17	2.42									
		2.11	3.06	3.25									
Order fillers	28	1.02	1.37	1.64	18 (1)	12	7 (2)	3	1	4 (1)	3	10	9
		1.40	2.18	2.39									
		1.71	2.73	2.90									
Receiving clerks	28	1.11	1.82	1.92	9	6	2	4	0	0	4	6	5 (1)
		1.53	2.29	2.51									
		1.81	2.75	3.03									
Truckers, power (fork lift)	34	1.00	1.75	1.85	21	10	14 (1)	5 (1)	5	5	9	15	12
		1.52	2.31	2.52									
		1.75	2.69	2.85									
Shipping and receiving clerks	26	1.21	1.68	1.87	8 (1)	7	2 (1)	2	2	1	4	3	1
		1.52	2.40	2.49									
		1.90	2.72	3.06									
Shipping clerks	28	1.22	1.79	1.86	8 (1)	10 (1)	6	5	1	1	3 (1)	8 (1)	3 (2)
		1.57	2.35	2.55									
		1.84	2.74	3.06									

See footnotes at end of table.

TABLE A–3c (continued)

Occupation (in order of ascending average earnings in 1963–1964)	No. of Areas in Group	Areas outside New England — Average Hourly Earnings Lowest, Median, Highest			Number of Areas outside New England with Average Hourly Earnings Below or Equal to Earnings in — BOSTON			PROVIDENCE			WORCESTER		
		1951–1952	1960–1961	1963–1964	1951–1952	1960–1961	1963–1964	1951–1952	1960–1961	1963–1964	1951–1952	1960–1961	1963–1964
Guards	23	$1.13	$1.70	$1.97									
		1.51	2.37	2.60	5 (2)	2	1	1	1	1	5	2	1
		1.77	2.70	2.95									
Truck drivers, medium (1½–4 tons)	30	1.00	1.47	1.60									
		1.56	2.43	2.66	17 (2)	16	16	6	6	7	6	6	4
		2.03	3.28	3.52									
Truckers, power (other than fork lift)	19	1.35	2.01	2.15									
		1.61	2.43	2.63	9 (4)	4	6	0	0	0	7	9	11
		1.80	2.86	2.96									
Truck drivers, heavy (over 4 tons, trailer type)	18	1.07	1.58	1.74									
		1.71	2.68	2.92	7 (2)	5	5	3	3	3	3	n.a.	n.a.
		2.04	3.18	3.47									

a For each occupation, areas are those for which data are available in all three time periods.

b Figures in parentheses indicate number of areas with earnings equal to earnings in Boston, Providence, or Worcester. Other figures indicate number of areas with lower earnings.

SOURCE: See Table A–3.

TABLE A-4

Average Weekly Earnings of Women in 16 Office Occupations in Manufacturing in Areas outside New England and in Boston, Providence, and Worcester, 1951–1952, 1960–1961, and 1963–1964

Occupation (in order of ascending average earnings in 1963–1964)	Number in Average	Areas outside New England Average[a]			Boston			Providence			Worcester		
		1951–1952	1960–1961	1963–1964	1951–1952	1960–1961	1963–1964	1951–1952	1960–1961	1963–1964	1951–1952	1960–1961	1963–1964
Office girls	12	$40.08	$61.92	$66.50	$40.00	$57.00	$59.50	$35.00	$46.00	$53.00	$39.00	$55.00	n.a.
Typists, class B	30	43.25	64.38	70.10	42.50	63.50	68.00	39.00	52.00	60.00	40.50	57.00	62.00
File clerks, class B	16	42.78	64.66	72.13	42.50	60.00	67.50	35.50	51.50	61.50	37.00	56.50	63.00
Switchboard operator-receptionists	32	46.83	69.02	75.16	44.50	67.00	74.00	42.00	60.00	66.00	44.00	63.00	70.00
Machine billers (billing machine)	15	49.10	70.23	76.07	45.00	66.00	71.00	44.00	64.00	68.50	43.50	72.50	n.a.
Transcribing-machine operators, general	19	48.21	72.37	78.03	47.00	67.00	70.50	41.00	61.50	72.00	44.50	68.50	n.a.
Order clerks	20	49.85	72.40	79.60	48.00	68.00	74.50	43.00	64.50	71.00	45.00	76.00	82.00
Stenographers, general	35	51.17	77.96	81.54	49.50	73.00	68.00	44.00	67.00	71.50	46.50	71.50	77.50
Typists, class A	29	49.74	77.45	83.66	48.50	68.50	74.00	44.00	61.50	70.50	50.50	67.00	69.50

See footnotes at end of table.

TABLE A–4 (*continued*)

Occupation (in order of ascending average earnings in 1963–1964)	Areas outside New England				Boston			Providence			Worcester		
	Number in Average	Average^a 1951–1952	1960–1961	1963–1964	1951–1952	1960–1961	1963–1964	1951–1952	1960–1961	1963–1964	1951–1952	1960–1961	1963–1964
File clerks, class A	13	$50.50	$75.35	$84.62	$47.50	$69.00	$78.50	$47.50	$61.50	$74.50	n.a.	$78.00	n.a.
Payroll clerks	32	51.63	77.50	84.81	49.00	69.50	76.50	45.00	66.50	72.50	45.50	69.50	74.50
Comptometer operators	24	50.75	77.33	84.92	47.00	65.50	74.50	44.50	69.50	77.50	44.50	72.00	81.00
Switchboard operators	22	52.11	80.23	87.61	53.50	73.00	83.50	46.00	57.50	66.50	44.00	71.50	77.00
Keypunch operators^b	25	50.14	76.96	89.22	45.00	68.50	77.00	40.00	63.00	78.00	44.50	66.50	71.00
Secretaries	34	60.88	91.04	100.47	58.50	83.00	93.50	52.00	77.00	86.00	58.00	86.00	95.00
Industrial nurses	27	62.13	99.09	108.00	60.00	87.50	97.50	56.00	77.50	89.50	57.00	88.50	94.50

a Average of weekly earnings for each occupation based on areas for which data are available in all three time periods.
b Data refer to general classification of keypunch operators in 1951–1952 and 1960–1961 and to class A keypunch operators in 1963–1964.

Sources: U.S. Bureau of Labor Statistics, *Wages and Related Benefits: 40 Labor Markets, 1951–1952* (Bulletin No. 1113) (Washington, D.C.: U.S. Government Printing Office, [1952]), Table A–1a.

———, *Wages and Related Benefits: 82 Labor Markets, 1960–61* (Bulletin No. 1285–83) (Washington, D.C.: U.S. Government Printing Office, 1961), Table A–2.

———, *Wages and Related Benefits*. Part I. *80 Metropolitan Areas, 1963–64* (Bulletin No. 1385–82) (Washington, D.C.: U.S. Government Printing Office, 1964), Table A–2.

TABLE A-4a

Average Weekly Earnings for 16 Office Occupations in Manufacturing in Boston, Providence, and Worcester Relative to Average Earnings in Areas outside New England, 1951–1952, 1960–1961, and 1963–1964

For each occupation and time period, average of weekly earnings in areas outside New England shown in Table A-4 = 100

Occupation (in order of ascending average earnings in 1963–1964)	Number of Areas in Average	BOSTON			PROVIDENCE			WORCESTER		
		1951–1952	1960–1961	1963–1964	1951–1952	1960–1961	1963–1964	1951–1952	1960–1961	1963–1964
Office girls	12	99.8	92.1	89.5	87.3	74.3	79.7	97.3	88.8	n.a.
Typists, class B	30	98.3	98.6	97.0	90.2	80.8	85.6	93.6	88.5	88.4
File clerks, class B	16	99.3	92.8	93.6	83.0	79.6	85.3	86.5	87.4	87.3
Switchboard operator-receptionists	32	95.0	97.1	98.5	89.7	86.9	87.8	94.0	91.3	93.1
Machine billers (billing machine)	15	91.6	94.0	93.3	89.6	91.1	90.0	88.6	103.2	n.a.
Transcribing-machine operators, general	19	97.5	92.6	90.3	85.0	85.0	92.3	92.3	94.7	n.a.
Order clerks	20	96.3	93.9	93.6	86.3	89.1	89.2	90.3	105.0	103.0

TABLE A–4a (*continued*)

Occupation (in order of ascending average earnings in 1963–1964)	Number of Areas in Average	BOSTON			PROVIDENCE			WORCESTER		
		1951–1952	1960–1961	1963–1964	1951–1952	1960–1961	1963–1964	1951–1952	1960–1961	1963–1964
Stenographers, general	35	96.7	93.6	95.7	86.0	85.9	87.7	90.9	91.7	95.0
Typists, class A	29	97.5	88.4	88.5	88.5	79.4	84.3	101.5	86.5	83.1
File clerks, class A	13	94.1	91.6	92.8	94.1	81.6	88.0	n.a.	103.5	n.a.
Payroll clerks	32	94.9	89.7	90.2	87.2	85.8	85.5	88.1	89.7	87.8
Comptometer operators	24	92.6	84.7	87.7	87.7	89.9	91.3	87.7	93.1	95.4
Switchboard operators	22	102.7	91.0	95.3	88.3	71.7	75.9	84.4	89.1	87.9
Keypunch operators[a]	25	89.7	89.0	86.3	79.8	81.9	87.4	88.8	86.4	79.6
Secretaries	34	96.1	91.2	93.1	85.4	84.6	85.6	95.3	94.5	94.6
Industrial nurses	27	96.6	88.3	90.3	90.1	78.2	82.9	91.7	89.3	87.5

[a] Data refer to general classification of keypunch operators in 1951–1952 and 1960–1961 and to class A keypunch operators in 1963–1964.

SOURCE: See Table A–4.

TABLE A–4b

Distribution of Earnings Relatives for 16 Office Occupations in Manufacturing: Occupations in Boston, Providence, and Worcester Classified According to Size of Earnings Relative to Earnings in Areas outside New England, 1951–1952, 1960–1961, and 1963–1964

Distribution of earnings relatives shown in Table A–4a

Size of Relative	BOSTON			PROVIDENCE			WORCESTER		
	1951–52	1960–61	1963–64	1951–52	1960–61	1963–64	1951–52	1960–61	1963–64
105 and over	—	—	—	—	—	—	—	1	—
100–104	2	—	—	—	—	—	1	2	1
95–99	10	2	4	5	2	—	2	2	3
90–94	4	10	9	9	6	3	6	4	1
85–89	—	4	3	2	4	9	5	7	5
80–84	—	—	—	—	2	3	1	—	2
75–79	—	—	—	—	2	1	—	—	—
70–74	—	—	—	—	—	—	—	—	—
TOTAL NUMBER OF OCCUPATIONS	16	16	16	16	16	16	15	16	12

SOURCE: See Table A–4.

TABLE A–4c

Average Weekly Earnings for 16 Office Occupations in Manufacturing: Lowest, Median, and Highest Earnings in Areas outside New England,[a] and Number of These Areas with Earnings Below or Equal[b] to Earnings in Boston, Providence, and Worcester, 1951–1952, 1960–1961, and 1963–1964

| Occupation (in order of ascending average earnings in 1963–1964) | No. of Areas in Group | | Areas outside New England — Average Weekly Earnings Lowest, Median, Highest | | Number of Areas outside New England with Average Weekly Earnings Below or Equal to Earnings in — | | | | | | | | |
		1951–1952	1960–1961	1963–1964	BOSTON 1951–1952	BOSTON 1960–1961	BOSTON 1963–1964	PROVIDENCE 1951–1952	PROVIDENCE 1960–1961	PROVIDENCE 1963–1964	WORCESTER 1951–1952	WORCESTER 1960–1961	WORCESTER 1963–1964
Office girls	12	$34.50	$50.00	$54.00	6 (1)	3	2	1 (1)	0	0	5 (1)	2	n.a.
		39.50	61.00	65.00									
		46.50	79.00	92.00									
Typists, class B	30	37.50	52.00	56.50	13 (3)	12 (1)	10 (2)	2 (1)	0 (1)	2	8	4	3
		42.50	64.50	68.75									
		52.00	81.00	91.00									
File clerks, class B	16	37.50	54.50	63.50	8 (2)	4	5	0	0	0	0	1 (1)	0
		42.25	64.75	71.00									
		48.50	75.00	91.50									
Switchboard operator-receptionists	32	40.00	53.00	57.50	6 (3)	10 (2)	15 (1)	4	1 (1)	1	6	3 (1)	5 (2)
		46.00	68.75	74.75									
		54.00	79.50	88.00									
Machine billers (billing machine)	15	44.00	57.00	60.50	1	4 (1)	3	0 (1)	4	2 (1)	0	7 (1)	n.a.
		49.50	72.50	77.00									
		53.00	80.50	87.50									

See footnotes at end of table.

TABLE A-4c (continued)

Occupation (in order of ascending average earnings in 1963–1964)	Areas outside New England				Number of Areas outside New England with Average Weekly Earnings Below or Equal to Earnings in								
	No. of Areas in Group	Average Weekly Earnings Lowest, Median, Highest			BOSTON			PROVIDENCE			WORCESTER		
		1951– 1952	1960– 1961	1963– 1964	1951– 1952	1960– 1961	1963– 1964	1951– 1952	1960– 1961	1963– 1964	1951– 1952	1960– 1961	1963– 1964
Transcribing-machine operators, general	19	$43.50 47.50 57.00	$65.50 69.50 89.50	$68.00 75.00 100.50	7 (2)	3 (2)	1	0	0	2	3 (1)	6 (3)	n.a.
Order clerks	20	45.50 49.25 56.50	51.50 72.50 86.50	64.00 78.00 94.00	7 (2)	5	4 (2)	0	1 (1)	1	0	15 (1)	14
Stenographers, general	35	43.50 51.00 60.50	59.00 78.00 95.50	68.50 81.50 97.00	12 (2)	9	12 (2)	1	1	1 (1)	2 (1)	6 (1)	12
Typists, class A	29	43.00 49.50 57.50	66.00 77.50 94.50	70.50 83.00 101.50	10 (1)	1	1	1	0	0 (1)	15 (2)	1	0
File clerks, class A	13	43.00 50.00 57.00	65.50 74.00 85.00	76.50 84.00 95.50	3 (1)	1	2 (1)	3 (1)	0	0	n.a.	8	n.a.
Payroll clerks	32	42.00 51.00 61.00	53.50 77.00 97.00	62.00 83.75 105.50	7 (4)	3	3 (2)	2	2	2	2	3	3
Comptometer operators	24	47.00 49.50 59.00	63.00 77.00 91.50	69.00 82.25 105.50	0 (4)	2 (1)	3	0	3	6	0	3 (1)	11

See footnotes at end of table.

TABLE A–4c *(continued)*

Occupation (in order of ascending average earnings in 1963–1964)	No. of Areas in Group	Areas outside New England — Average Weekly Earnings — Lowest, Median, Highest 1951–1952	1960–1961	1963–1964	Boston 1951–1952	Boston 1960–1961	Boston 1963–1964	Providence 1951–1952	Providence 1960–1961	Providence 1963–1964	Worcester 1951–1952	Worcester 1960–1961	Worcester 1963–1964
Switchboard operators	22	$45.50 / 51.50 / 58.50	$71.00 / 79.75 / 94.00	$77.00 / 87.50 / 103.00	13 (2)	2	3 (4)	1	0	0	0	1	0 (1)
Keypunch operators[c]	25	44.50 / 49.50 / 57.00	64.50 / 77.50 / 93.00	78.00 / 88.50 / 106.00	2 (1)	2	0	0	0	0 (1)	0 (2)	0	0
Secretaries	34	50.50 / 61.00 / 71.00	74.50 / 90.75 / 111.00	85.00 / 100.25 / 123.00	7 (2)	4 (1)	6	1	2	1	7	6	8
Industrial nurses	27	52.50 / 61.50 / 70.00	90.50 / 98.50 / 113.00	99.00 / 107.50 / 121.00	5 (1)	0	0	1	0	0	1	0	0

Heading for the right-hand block: Number of Areas outside New England with Average Weekly Earnings Below or Equal to Earnings in (Boston, Providence, Worcester).

[a] For each occupation, areas are those for which data are available in all three time periods.

[b] Figures in parentheses indicate number of areas with earnings equal to earnings in Boston, Providence, or Worcester. Other figures indicate number of areas with lower earnings.

[c] Data refer to general classification of keypunch operators in 1951–1952 and 1960–1961 and to class A keypunch operators in 1963–1964.

SOURCE: See Table A–4.

TABLE A–5

Metropolitan Areas outside New England Used in
Wage Comparisons with Boston, Hartford, and Worcester:
Production Occupations in Machinery Manufacturing
(Table A–6)
1953–1954, 1961, and 1964

Middle Atlantic	*Middle West*
Newark–Jersey City	Chicago
New York	Cleveland
Philadelphia	Detroit
Pittsburgh	Milwaukee
	Minneapolis–St. Paul
	St. Louis
South	*Far West*
Baltimore	Denver
Dallas	Los Angeles–Long Beach
Houston	Portland
	San Francisco–Oakland

SOURCE: U.S. Bureau of Labor Statistics, *Wages and Related Benefits in the Machinery Industry: Postwar Wage Trends. Survey of 20 Labor Markets, 1953–54* (Bulletin No. 1160) (Washington, D. C.: U.S. Government Printing Office, [1954]).

TABLE A–6

Average Straight-Time Hourly Earnings of Men in 28 Production Occupations in Machinery Manufacturing in Areas outside New England and in Boston, Hartford, and Worcester, 1953–1954, 1961, and 1964

Occupation (in order of ascending average earnings in 1964)	Number in Average	Areas outside New England Average[a]			Boston			Hartford			Worcester		
		1953–1954	1961	1964	1953–1954	1961	1964	1953–1954	1961	1964	1953–1954	1961	1964
Janitors, porters, cleaners	17	$1.50	$1.98	$2.13	$1.33	$1.76	$1.91	$1.42	$1.93	$2.18	$1.44	$1.89	$1.96
Drill-press operators, spindle, class C	10	1.61	2.14	2.24	1.57	1.86	2.02	1.68	2.28	2.68	1.55	1.96	2.23
Assemblers, class C	13	1.64	2.13	2.26	1.49	1.93	2.18	1.63	1.97	2.31	1.57	2.13	2.23
Machine-tool operators, production, class C[b]	16	1.66	2.16	2.31	1.49	1.89	1.97	1.74	2.45	2.71	1.59	2.05	2.19
Laborers, material handling	15	1.58	2.14	2.34	1.42	2.02	2.12	1.46	2.03	2.15	1.59	2.01	2.18
Assemblers, class B	16	1.85	2.41	2.63	1.73	2.34	2.54	1.72	2.32	2.46	1.80	2.29	2.53
Welders, hand, class B	10	1.86	2.42	2.66	1.78	n.a.	2.58	n.a.	2.10	2.66	1.81	2.34	2.78
Drill-press operators, radial, class B	11	1.88	2.45	2.66	1.70	2.23	2.44	1.79	2.38	2.52	1.69	2.23	2.54
Grinding-machine operators, class B	10	1.94	2.47	2.72	1.73	2.26	2.47	1.92	2.54	2.72	1.88	2.36	2.50
Machine-tool operators, production, class B[c]	17	1.89	2.53	2.72	1.69	2.29	2.41	1.81	2.52	2.71	1.79	2.33	2.54

See footnotes at end of table.

TABLE A-6 (continued)

Occupation (in order of ascending average earnings in 1964)	Areas outside New England	Average[a]			Boston			Hartford			Worcester		
	Number in Average	1953– 1954	1961	1964	1953– 1954	1961	1964	1953– 1954	1961	1964	1953– 1954	1961	1964
Drill-press operators, spindle, class B	12	$1.84	$2.47	$2.73	$1.65	$2.19	$2.39	n.a.	$2.50	$2.65	$1.70	n.a.	$2.56
Inspectors, class B	12	1.88	2.54	2.74	1.70	2.37	2.42	1.70	2.36	2.57	1.74	2.46	2.65
Turret-lathe operators, hand, class B	17	1.90	2.54	2.77	1.71	2.26	2.39	1.82	2.55	2.76	1.71	2.33	2.45
Milling-machine operators, class B	10	1.93	2.49	2.79	1.71	2.47	2.53	1.68	2.40	2.59	1.85	2.32	2.56
Engine-lathe operators, class B	10	1.95	2.64	2.84	1.72	2.33	2.54	1.74	2.31	2.45	1.71	2.22	2.43
Drill-press operators, spindle, class A	9	2.07	2.61	2.93	2.19	2.85	2.93	1.95	2.53	2.96	1.88	2.50	2.93
Welders, hand, class A	17	2.13	2.75	3.02	1.87	2.49	2.71	2.11	2.88	3.15	1.83	2.65	2.91
Assemblers, class A	17	2.10	2.78	3.02	1.98	2.70	2.88	2.06	2.71	2.89	2.02	2.62	2.79
Turret-lathe operators, hand, class A	16	2.14	2.80	3.04	1.94	2.58	2.72	2.06	2.71	2.94	1.95	2.44	2.73
Inspectors, class A	16	2.13	2.84	3.05	1.93	2.66	2.84	1.90	2.44	2.77	1.90	2.52	2.71
Milling-machine operators, class A	14	2.16	2.82	3.06	2.10	2.79	2.92	2.07	2.76	3.02	1.90	2.51	2.84
Drill-press operators, radial, class A	15	2.12	2.82	3.07	2.06	2.68	2.87	2.05	2.55	3.04	1.87	2.39	2.72

See footnotes at end of table.

TABLE A-6 *(continued)*

Occupation (in order of ascending average earnings in 1964)	Areas outside New England				BOSTON			HARTFORD			WORCESTER		
	Number in Average	Average[a]			1953–1954	1961	1964	1953–1954	1961	1964	1953–1954	1961	1964
		1953–1954	1961	1964									
Engine-lathe operators, class A	15	$2.20	$2.86	$3.07	$1.95	$2.64	$2.79	$2.03	$2.70	$2.95	$1.88	$2.55	$2.63
Grinding-machine operators, class A	15	2.21	2.83	3.08	2.05	2.69	2.84	2.15	2.74	3.07	2.02	2.57	2.70
Machine-tool operators, production, class A[d]	17	2.16	2.84	3.08	2.01	2.64	2.83	2.06	2.71	3.02	1.96	2.52	2.76
Machine-tool operators, toolroom	14	2.15	2.93	3.17	1.91	2.54	2.75	2.13	2.93	2.98	1.96	2.43	2.70
Electricians, maintenance	15	2.19	2.95	3.20	2.04	2.70	3.06	2.11	2.76	3.09	1.95	2.59	2.88
Tool and die makers (other than jobbing)	16	2.34	3.11	3.36	2.10	2.87	3.16	2.21	2.88	3.16	2.07	2.68	2.89

[a] Average of hourly earnings for each occupation based on areas for which data are available in all three time periods.
[b] A general job classification, including other class C occupations in addition to those shown separately in this table.
[c] A general job classification, including other class B occupations in addition to those shown separately in this table.
[d] A general job classification, including other class A occupations in addition to those shown separately in this table.

SOURCES: U.S Bureau of Labor Statistics, *Wages and Related Benefits in the Machinery Industries: Postwar Wage Trends. Survey of 20 Labor Markets, 1953–54* (Bulletin No. 1160) (Washington, D.C.: U.S. Government Printing Office, [1954]), Table 1A.

———, *Industry Wage Survey: Machinery Manufacturing, March–May 1961* (Bulletin No. 1309) (Washington, D.C.: U.S. Government Printing Office, 1961), Table A–1.

———, *Industry Wage Survey: Machinery Manufacturing, March–May 1964* (Bulletin No. 1429) (Washington, D.C.: U.S. Government Printing Office, 1965), Table 1.

TABLE A–6a

Average Hourly Earnings for 28 Production Occupations in Machinery Manufacturing in Boston, Hartford, and Worcester Relative to Average Earnings in Areas outside New England, 1953–1954, 1961, and 1964

For each occupation and time period, average of hourly earnings in areas outside New England shown in Table A–6 = 100

Occupation (in order of ascending average earnings in 1964)	Number of Areas in Average	BOSTON			HARTFORD			WORCESTER		
		1953–1954	1961	1964	1953–1954	1961	1964	1953–1954	1961	1964
Janitors, porters, cleaners	17	88.7	88.9	89.7	94.7	97.5	102.3	96.0	95.5	92.0
Drill-press operators, spindle, class C	10	97.5	86.9	90.2	104.3	106.5	119.6	96.3	91.6	99.6
Assemblers, class C	13	90.9	90.6	96.5	99.4	92.5	102.2	95.7	100.0	98.7
Machine-tool operators, production, class C[a]	16	89.8	87.5	85.3	104.8	113.4	117.3	95.8	94.9	94.8
Laborers, material handling	15	89.9	94.4	90.6	92.4	94.9	91.9	100.6	93.9	93.2
Assemblers, class B	16	93.5	97.1	96.6	93.0	96.3	93.5	97.3	95.0	96.2
Welders, hand, class B	10	95.7	n.a.	97.0	n.a.	86.8	100.0	97.3	96.7	104.5
Drill-press operators, radial, class B	11	90.4	91.0	91.7	95.2	97.1	94.7	89.9	91.0	95.5
Grinding-machine operators, class B	10	89.2	91.5	90.8	99.0	102.8	100.0	96.9	95.5	91.9
Machine-tool operators, production, class B[b]	17	89.4	90.5	88.6	95.8	99.6	99.6	94.7	92.1	93.4

See footnotes at end of table.

TABLE A–6a (continued)

Occupation (in order of ascending average earnings in 1964)	Number of Areas in Average	Boston			Hartford			Worcester		
		1953–1954	1961	1964	1953–1954	1961	1964	1953–1954	1961	1964
Drill-press operators, spindle, class B	12	89.7	88.7	87.5	n.a.	101.2	97.1	92.4	n.a.	93.8
Inspectors, class B	12	90.4	93.3	88.3	90.4	92.9	93.8	92.6	96.9	96.7
Turret-lathe operators, hand, class B	17	90.0	89.0	86.3	95.8	100.4	99.6	90.0	91.7	88.4
Milling-machine operators, class B	10	88.6	99.2	90.7	87.0	96.4	92.8	95.9	93.2	91.8
Engine-lathe operators, class B	10	88.2	88.3	89.4	89.2	87.5	86.3	87.7	84.1	85.6
Drill-press operators, spindle, class A	9	105.8	109.2	100.0	94.2	96.9	101.0	90.8	95.8	100.0
Welders, hand, class A	17	87.8	90.5	89.7	99.1	104.7	104.3	85.9	96.4	96.4
Assemblers, class A	17	94.3	97.1	95.4	98.1	97.5	95.7	96.2	94.2	92.4
Turret-lathe operators, hand, class A	16	90.7	92.1	89.5	96.3	96.8	96.7	91.1	87.1	89.8
Inspectors, class A	16	90.6	93.7	93.1	89.2	85.9	90.8	89.2	88.7	88.9
Milling-machine operators, class A	14	97.2	98.9	95.4	95.8	97.9	98.7	88.0	89.0	92.8

See footnotes at end of table.

TABLE A–6a *(continued)*

Occupation (in order of ascending average earnings in 1964)	Number of Areas in Average	BOSTON 1953–1954	BOSTON 1961	BOSTON 1964	HARTFORD 1953–1954	HARTFORD 1961	HARTFORD 1964	WORCESTER 1953–1954	WORCESTER 1961	WORCESTER 1964
Drill-press operators, radial, class A	15	97.2	95.0	93.5	96.7	90.4	99.0	88.2	84.8	88.6
Engine-lathe operators, class A	15	88.6	92.3	90.9	92.3	94.4	96.1	85.5	89.2	85.7
Grinding-machine operators, class A	15	92.8	95.1	92.2	97.3	96.8	99.7	91.4	90.8	87.7
Machine-tool operators, production, class A[c]	17	93.1	93.0	91.9	95.4	95.4	98.1	90.7	88.7	89.6
Machine-tool operators, toolroom	14	88.8	86.7	86.8	99.1	100.0	94.0	91.2	82.9	85.2
Electricians, maintenance	15	93.2	91.5	95.6	96.3	93.6	96.6	89.0	87.8	90.0
Tool and die makers (other than jobbing)	16	89.7	92.3	94.0	94.4	92.6	94.0	88.5	86.2	86.0

[a] A general job classification, including other class C occupations in addition to those shown separately in this table.
[b] A general job classification, including other class B occupations in addition to those shown separately in this table.
[c] A general job classification, including other class A occupations in addition to those shown separately in this table.

SOURCE: See Table A–6.

TABLE A–6b

Distribution of Earnings Relatives for 28 Production Occupations in Machinery Manufacturing:
Occupations in Boston, Hartford, and Worcester Classified According to Size
of Earnings Relative to Earnings in Areas outside New England,
1953–1954, 1961, and 1964

Distribution of earnings relatives shown in Table A–6a

Size of Relative	Boston			Hartford			Worcester		
	1953–54	1961	1964	1953–54	1961	1964	1953–54	1961	1964
105 and over	1	1	—	1	3	2	—	—	1
100–104	—	—	1	1	5	9	1	1	2
95–99	4	6	6	15	11	9	10	8	6
90–94	15	13	14	6	6	7	9	8	11
85–89	8	7	7	3	3	1	8	8	8
80–84	—	—	—	—	—	—	—	2	—
75–79	—	—	—	—	—	—	—	—	—
70–74	—	—	—	—	—	—	—	—	—
TOTAL NUMBER OF OCCUPATIONS	28	27	28	26	28	28	28	27	28

SOURCE: See Table A–6.

TABLE A–6c

Average Hourly Earnings for 28 Production Occupations in Machinery Manufacturing: Lowest, Median, and Highest Earnings in Areas outside New England[a] and Number of These Areas with Earnings Below or Equal[b] to Earnings in Boston, Hartford, and Worcester, 1953–1954, 1961, and 1964

Occupation (in order of ascending average earnings in 1964)	No. of Areas in Group	Areas outside New England — Average Hourly Earnings: Lowest, Median, Highest 1953–1954	1961	1964	Number of Areas outside New England with Average Hourly Earnings Below or Equal to Earnings in — BOSTON 1953–1954	BOSTON 1961	BOSTON 1964	HARTFORD 1953–1954	HARTFORD 1961	HARTFORD 1964	WORCESTER 1953–1954	WORCESTER 1961	WORCESTER 1964
Janitors, porters, cleaners	17	$1.15	$1.47	$1.57	2	2	2 (1)	4	7	9 (1)	5 (1)	5	3 (1)
		1.50	1.97	2.12									
		1.78	2.34	2.47									
Drill-press operators, spindle, class C	10	1.23	1.57	1.63	2 (1)	2	2	7	5	9	2	2	4 (1)
		1.62	2.23	2.29									
		1.87	2.49	2.76									
Assemblers, class C	13	1.25	1.43	1.56	4	2	5	5 (1)	2	6	5	8 (1)	5
		1.67	2.10	2.33									
		1.95	2.54	2.85									
Machine-tool operators, production, class C[c]	16	1.34	1.67	1.76	3 (1)	2	1	11	15	16	5 (1)	3 (1)	5
		1.69	2.16	2.33									
		1.93	2.51	2.67									
Laborers, material handling	15	1.17	1.42	1.66	2	2 (1)	3	2	3	3 (1)	7	2	4
		1.60	2.10	2.40									
		1.83	2.53	2.82									
Assemblers, class B	16	1.49	1.74	1.99	2 (1)	8 (1)	7	2	8	5	6 (1)	5 (1)	6 (1)
		1.84	2.33	2.65									
		2.14	2.79	3.00									

See footnotes at end of table.

TABLE A–6c *(continued)*

Occupation (in order of ascending average earnings in 1964)	No. of Areas in Group	Areas outside New England — Average Hourly Earnings Lowest, Median, Highest 1953–1954	1961	1964	Number of Areas outside New England with Average Hourly Earnings Below or Equal to Earnings in — BOSTON 1953–1954	1961	1964	HARTFORD 1953–1954	1961	1964	WORCESTER 1953–1954	1961	1964
Welders, hand, class B	10	$1.50 / 1.91 / 2.06	$1.84 / 2.46 / 2.73	$2.00 / 2.71 / 3.08	2	n.a.	4	n.a.	1	4	2	2 (1)	6
Drill-press operators, radial, class B	11	1.46 / 1.95 / 2.06	1.84 / 2.48 / 2.70	2.13 / 2.66 / 3.01	1	1	1	3	4	2	1	1	2 (2)
Grinding-machine operators, class B	10	1.54 / 2.00 / 2.21	1.89 / 2.49 / 2.74	2.08 / 2.79 / 3.04	1	1	1	4	6	4	4	3	1 (1)
Machine-tool operators, production, class B[d]	17	1.58 / 1.92 / 2.05	2.00 / 2.58 / 2.73	2.11 / 2.79 / 2.94	2	2	1	3 (1)	6	7	3	2	2
Drill-press operators, spindle, class B	12	1.53 / 1.84 / 2.01	2.05 / 2.46 / 2.73	2.36 / 2.76 / 3.14	1	1	1	n.a.	7	5	1	n.a.	4
Inspectors, class B	12	1.53 / 1.91 / 2.05	1.95 / 2.63 / 2.82	2.20 / 2.75 / 2.97	2	3	1	2	3	1	2	4	3
Turret-lathe operators, hand, class B	17	1.61 / 1.91 / 2.04	2.01 / 2.51 / 2.90	2.08 / 2.81 / 3.04	2	1	1	4	9 (1)	7	2	2	1

See footnotes at end of table.

Occupation (in order of ascending average earnings in 1964)	No. of Areas in Group	Average Hourly Earnings — Lowest, Median, Highest 1954	1961	1964	BOSTON 1954	1961	1964	HARTFORD 1954	1961	1964	WORCESTER 1954	1961	1964
Milling-machine operators, class B	10	$1.79	$2.21	$2.42	0	5	1	0	5	1	2	2	1
		1.93	2.43	2.87									
		2.08	2.74	3.01									
Engine-lathe operators, class B	10	1.77	2.36	2.61	0	0	0	0	0	0	0	0	0
		1.94	2.61	2.79									
		2.18	2.98	3.20									
Drill-press operators, spindle, class A	9	1.80	2.40	2.64	7	7	5	2	5	5	2	5	5
		2.12	2.49	2.92									
		2.23	2.94	3.27									
Welders, hand, class A	17	1.76	2.22	2.43	1	1	1	5	12	12 (1)	1	4	4
		2.14	2.78	3.07									
		2.36	3.05	3.38									
Assemblers, class A	17	1.71	2.16	2.47	4 (1)	6	4	6 (1)	6	4	5	4	3
		2.14	2.79	3.04									
		2.43	3.19	3.40									
Turret-lathe operators, hand, class A	16	1.80	2.34	2.55	1	1	1	3	4	4	1 (1)	1	1
		2.14	2.81	3.06									
		2.41	3.06	3.38									
Inspectors, class A	16	1.85	2.41	2.67	1	2 (1)	1	1	1	1	1	1	1
		2.14	2.82	3.05									
		2.46	3.25	3.37									
Milling-machine operators, class A	14	1.87	2.34	2.58	5	7	4	3	7	5 (2)	2	1	1 (1)
		2.16	2.80	3.07									
		2.64	3.21	3.42									

Areas outside New England

Number of Areas outside New England with Average Hourly Earnings Below or Equal to Earnings in

See footnotes at end of table.

TABLE A–6c *(continued)*

Occupation (in order of ascending average earnings in 1964)	No. of Areas in Group	Areas outside New England Average Hourly Earnings Lowest, Median, Highest 1953–1954	1961	1964	Number of Areas outside New England with Average Hourly Earnings Below or Equal to Earnings in — BOSTON 1953–1954	BOSTON 1961	BOSTON 1964	HARTFORD 1953–1954	HARTFORD 1961	HARTFORD 1964	WORCESTER 1953–1954	WORCESTER 1961	WORCESTER 1964
Drill-press operators, radial, class A	15	$1.82 / 2.13 / 2.65	$2.62 / 2.80 / 3.09	$2.77 / 3.08 / 3.47	7	3	3 (1)	7	0	6	1	0	0
Engine-lathe operators, class A	15	1.90 / 2.20 / 2.66	2.48 / 2.80 / 3.22	2.64 / 3.09 / 3.43	1	2	1 (1)	1	4	4	0	1	0
Grinding-machine operators, class A	15	1.86 / 2.26 / 2.68	2.44 / 2.89 / 3.24	2.66 / 3.15 / 3.44	2	5	3	5	5	6	2	2	1
Machine-tool operators, production, class A[e]	17	1.80 / 2.20 / 2.66	2.35 / 2.85 / 3.19	2.59 / 3.08 / 3.50	2	2	2	4	5	7	2	1	1
Machine-tool operators, toolroom	14	1.83 / 2.19 / 2.44	2.49 / 2.92 / 3.58	2.82 / 3.14 / 3.65	2	1	0	5 (1)	7 (1)	3	2	0	0
Electricians, maintenance	15	1.78 / 2.22 / 2.47	2.41 / 2.97 / 3.34	2.61 / 3.18 / 3.68	2	1 (1)	3	3	2	3	2	1	2
Tool and die makers (other than jobbing)	16	1.97 / 2.35 / 2.57	2.65 / 3.12 / 3.53	2.88 / 3.34 / 3.88	1	2	3	3	2 (1)	3 (1)	1	1	1

[a] For each occupation, areas are those for which data are available in all three time periods.

[b] Figures in parentheses indicate number of areas with earnings equal to earnings in Boston, Hartford, or Worcester. Other figures indicate number of areas with lower earnings.

[c] A general job classification, including other class C occupations in addition to those shown separately in this table.

[d] A general job classification, including other class B occupations in addition to those shown separately in this table.

[e] A general job classification, including other class A occupations in addition to those shown separately in this table.

APPENDIX B

COMPARING SOURCES OF WAGE AND SALARY INFORMATION

C HAPTERS III and V analyze various estimates of relative wage levels in each sector of New England's economy. This Appendix comments on the probable accuracy of each of these estimates. The general conclusion is that data from specialized statistical sources, such as the Census of Manufactures, the Census of Business, and Community Wage Surveys, are more accurate than the figures for earnings per person employed presented in Table 7 of Chapter III. The latter figures are calculated from the employment statistics of the Decennial Census and the personal income data of the U.S. Office of Business Economics, the only comprehensive personal income data available.

THE CENSUS OF MANUFACTURES

Table B–1 shows relative manufacturing wage rates in 1958 and 1963 in each New England state, Fairfield County, Connecticut, New England, and New England exclusive of Fairfield County. This information is based on a 100 per cent survey of manufacturing plants and is probably very accurate. Furthermore, wage and salary data for the year and employment data for various months during the year are collected on the same form, encouraging the provision of consistent information.

Chapter III has shown that wage rates are relatively low in New England in most manufacturing industries. Comparisons of wage levels based on average manufacturing wage rates, however, could be misleading if no allowances were made for the varying levels of skills in different regions. Occupational skill data in the Decennial Census

TABLE B–1

Average Hourly and Annual Earnings per Person Employed in Manufacturing in the New England States, Fairfield County, Conn., New England, and New England Excluding Fairfield County, Relative to Earnings in the United States, 1958 and 1963

U.S. = 100

Area	1958		1963	
	Average Hourly Earnings for Production Workers	Annual Earnings per Manufacturing Employee[a]	Average Hourly Earnings for Production Workers	Annual Earnings per Manufacturing Employee[a]
Connecticut	101.8	103.0	103.1	105.9
Fairfield County	103.2	105.3	105.0	108.1[b]
Maine	78.5	79.7	77.6	75.9
Massachusetts	90.9	92.8	93.3	93.3
New Hampshire	79.0	78.0	79.4	78.0
Rhode Island	81.7	82.1	82.0	81.2
Vermont	83.6	85.0	85.8	85.7
NEW ENGLAND	91.3	92.8	92.8	93.6
NEW ENGLAND (excluding Fairfield County, Conn.)	90.4	91.8	91.8	92.4

[a] Data for operating manufacturing establishments, excluding central administrative offices and auxiliary units.

[b] Operating manufacturing data for Fairfield County for 1963 estimated to be same proportion of total manufacturing establishment data as in Connecticut.

SOURCES: U.S. Bureau of the Census, *U.S. Census of Manufactures: 1958.* Vol. III. *Area Statistics* (Washington, D.C.: U.S. Government Printing Office, 1961).

——, *Census of Manufactures: 1963. General Statistics for Industry Groups and Industries* (Preliminary Report MC63[P]–3*) (Washington, D.C.: U.S. Government Printing Office, October, 1965).

——, *Census of Manufactures: 1963* (Preliminary Reports MC63[P]–S7, –S20, –S22, –S30, –S40, –S46) (Washington, D.C.: U.S. Government Printing Office, 1965).

suggest that the level of skill in New England is no lower than that in the United States. Thus the Census of Manufactures data clearly demonstrate that New England manufacturing wage rates were relatively low in both 1958 and 1963.

THE CENSUS OF BUSINESS

Table B–2 shows the relative wage levels in 1958 and 1963 for trade and selected services employment in each New England state, Fairfield County, Connecticut, New England, and New England exclusive of Fairfield County. The Census of Business also provides 100 per cent coverage. Furthermore, wage and salary data for the year and employment data for the work week ended nearest November 15 are collected on the same form.

The Census of Business data may have two weaknesses for use in interarea comparisons, however.

1. *November employment has a different seasonal variation in different areas.* Comparisons of annual earnings per employee, *as of November 15,* can be misleading. In Table B–2, however, the employment data have been adjusted by the November seasonal adjustment factors for full-time nonagricultural employment used by the U.S. Bureau of Labor Statistics for the United States and by the Federal Reserve Bank of Boston for New England. The latter figure was also used to adjust the trade employment data for each New England state and for Fairfield County.

2. *No allowance is made for the varying skill levels of the work force in different areas.* Table B–2 suggests that trade earnings per employee in New England, exclusive of Fairfield County, Connecticut, were 97.9 per cent and 100.4 per cent of the national average in 1958 and 1963. However, these data significantly overestimate the relative level of earnings of trade employees in the region. As is shown in Table B–3, trade employment in the region is at a significantly higher skill level than that in the nation.

UNITED STATES BUREAU OF LABOR STATISTICS COMMUNITY WAGE SURVEYS

The interarea pay comparisons in Table 4 in Chapter III are based on a collection of hourly rates for specific jobs in eighty metropolitan areas throughout the country. The manufacturing wage data shown in

TABLE B–2

Annual Earnings per Person Employed in Trade and Selected Services in the New England States, Fairfield County, Conn., New England, and New England Excluding Fairfield County, Relative to Earnings in the United States, 1958 and 1963

U.S. = 100

Area	1958		1963	
	Annual Earnings per Trade Employee[a]	Annual Earnings per Employee in Selected Services	Annual Earnings per Trade Employee[b]	Annual Earnings per Employee in Selected Services
Connecticut	103.5	99.8	105.6	95.7
Fairfield County	107.1	106.4	111.2	106.9
Maine	87.0	74.2	89.8	89.7
Massachusetts	100.4	94.7	102.8	99.6
New Hampshire	88.3	87.2	90.1	99.2
Rhode Island	93.1	83.9	97.6	88.8
Vermont	85.7	78.5	88.4	86.8
NEW ENGLAND	98.5	92.4	101.1	96.8
NEW ENGLAND (excluding Fairfield County, Conn.)	97.9	91.5	100.4	96.1

[a] Based on November 15 employment, seasonally adjusted (U.S. = 102.08, New England = 101.3).
[b] Based on November 15 employment, seasonally adjusted (U.S. = 102.1, New England = 100.5).

SOURCES: U.S. Bureau of the Census, *County and City Data Book, 1962: A Statistical Abstract Supplement* (Washington, D.C.: U.S. Government Printing Office, 1962), Tables 1 and 2.

———, *Census of Business: 1963. Retail Trade: United States Summary*; BC63–RA1; *Connecticut*: BC63–RA8 (Preprints) (Washington, D.C.: U.S. Government Printing Office, 1965), Tables 3 and 4.

———, *Census of Business: 1963. Wholesale Trade: United States Summary*: BC63–WA1; *Connecticut*: BC63–WA8 (Preprints) (Washington, D.C.: U.S. Government Printing Office, 1965), Tables 4 and 5.

———, *Census of Business: 1963. Selected Services: United States Summary*: BC63–SA1; *Connecticut*: BC63–SA8 (Preprints) (Washington, D.C.: U.S. Government Printing Office, 1965), Tables 3 and 4.

TABLE B–3

*Occupational Distribution of Wage and Salaried Workers
in Trade in New England and the United States,
1960*

Classification of Occupations	New England (Percentage of Employment)	United States (Percentage of Employment)
Professional	2.4	2.1
Technicians	.1	.1
Managerial[a]	11.4	10.2
Craftsmen	9.3	8.3
Sales	34.9	30.5
Clerical	16.9	15.5
Bookkeepers	3.7	3.1
Cashiers	3.5	3.2
Operatives	13.7	13.5
Services	7.8	15.6
Charwomen, Janitors, Porters	.6	1.1
Laborers	3.5	4.2
TOTAL	100.0[b]	100.0[b]

[a] Does not include self-employed.

[b] Detail may not add to total due to rounding.

SOURCES: U.S. Bureau of the Census, *U.S. Census of Population: 1960. Detailed Characteristics.* Connecticut, Maine, Massachusetts, New Hampshire, Rhode Island, and Vermont (separate publication for each state) (Series PC[1]) (Washington, D.C.: U.S. Government Printing Office, 1962), Table 125. ————, *U.S. Census of Population: 1960. Supplementary Reports. Industry Group by Occupation: 1960* (Series PC[S1]–27) (Washington, D.C.: U.S. Government Printing Office, 1962).

Table 4 are entirely consistent with the 1963 Census of Manufactures wage data. The data for "nonmanufacturing" wages cover such a broad area that they cannot be compared with any other published series.

The strength of these data is that metropolitan area wage comparisons are based on a specific set of jobs in both manufacturing and nonmanufacturing. The weakness of the data is their coverage, for the sample includes only a selected group of jobs. Most production workers are excluded, as are government workers. The survey does not cover rural areas or smaller cities.

RELATIVE WAGE AND SALARY ESTIMATES BASED ON EMPLOYMENT
DATA FROM THE U.S. BUREAU OF LABOR STATISTICS AND WAGE AND
SALARY DATA FROM THE U.S. OFFICE OF BUSINESS ECONOMICS

Table B–4 provides relative wage and salary estimates for each
New England state and for New England based on annual state
personal income statistics of the U.S. Office of Business Economics
and monthly labor-force estimates for each state produced by the
U.S. Bureau of Labor Statistics. Except for agriculture, both agencies
provide data for each major labor-force sector (for example, manufacturing, trade, services, government). Most of the basic data for
both series are collected and coded by the U.S. Bureau of Employment
Security. The wage and salary data are based largely on records of
employers reporting under laws relating to unemployment insurance.
These employers in 1950 accounted for 93 per cent of total wages
and salaries paid in covered industries in the United States.

New England–United States comparisons based on these data have
a number of possible disadvantages, despite their common source.

1. *The published wage and salary components of personal income for the State of Connecticut have been adjusted upward (by
about 7 per cent for 1960) by the U.S. Office of Business Economics,
so as to account for income earned by Connecticut residents commuting into New York City. On the other hand, the Connecticut employment data of the U.S. Bureau of Labor Statistics exclude com-
muters.*

To make the U.S. Office of Business Economics and the U.S.
Bureau of Labor Statistics series more comparable (in Table B–4),
the Connecticut wage and salary payments in each employment sector
have been reduced to their original levels.

2. *The employment data of the Bureau of Labor Statistics are
collected for the middle week of each month by a sampling procedure.*

Although these data can be converted into annual average figures
for each employment sector, the resulting information is much more
accurate for total nonagricultural employment than it is for each
employment sector.

3. *There is some double counting of employees in the U.S.
Bureau of Labor Statistics data. If an individual has a full-time job
and a part-time job, he is counted as two employees.*

Double counting may or may not create a bias in the resulting

*Annual Wages and Salaries per Employee in Nonagricultural Industries
in New England, New England Excluding Connecticut, and the New England States,
Relative to the United States Average, 1960*

U.S. = 100

Industry (civilian)	New England[a]	New England Excluding Conn.	Conn.[a]	Maine	Mass.	N.H.	R.I.	Vt.
Total nonagricultural	95.9	92.5	106.3	83.6[c]	95.7	83.0[c]	88.4	85.4
Construction	99.6[b]	93.9	111.2[b]	85.5	95.3	88.5	99.2	92.3
Manufacturing	92.7	88.1	104.6	76.1	92.9	77.4	80.2	81.5
Trade	96.9	94.9	103.7	85.0	97.6	84.3	95.2	85.7
Finance, insurance, real estate	103.1	101.6	107.0	90.3	103.4	92.1	101.8	98.7
Transportation, communication, public utilities	93.9	93.3	96.1	88.9	94.6	92.9	94.4	87.8
Services, mining, misc.	93.5[b]	90.9	103.0[b]	89.2	94.7	77.5	76.8	82.7
Government	99.4	97.9	105.5	93.4[d]	99.3	93.4[d]	101.0	90.9

[a] Wages and salaries adjusted to exclude amounts earned by Connecticut residents commuting to New York, per U.S. Office of Business Economics.

[b] Mining included in "Construction," for Connecticut only.

[c] Excluding government. These adjustments made in Maine and New Hampshire only, not in New England totals.

[d] Average of Maine and New Hampshire combined, because of difficulty of assigning income and employment at Portsmouth Naval Base.

SOURCES: Robert E. Graham, Jr., and Edwin J. Coleman, "Consumer Incomes Up in All Regions in 1960," *Survey of Current Business*, XLI (August, 1961), 14–15.

U.S. Bureau of Labor Statistics, *Employment and Earnings Statistics for the United States: 1909–1960* (Bulletin No. 1312) (Washington, D.C.: U.S. Government Printing Office, 1961).

Unpublished employment data for the New England states furnished by U.S. Bureau of Labor Statistics, New England Regional Office, Boston, Mass.

estimates of relative earnings per employee in each region. It will not if the relative amount of double counting and the average number of hours worked are the same in each employment category in each geographical area.

As mentioned in Chapter III, however, it is likely that there are proportionately more multiple-job holders in New England than in the nation. Thus, when New England's total earnings are divided by its total employees, the result as shown in Table B–4 is probably an underestimate of the relative earnings of full-time employees in the region.

Nevertheless, the manufacturing and trade relatives are quite close to and consistent with those of the Census of Manufactures (Table B–1) and the Census of Business (Table B–2).

RELATIVE WAGE AND SALARY ESTIMATES BASED ON EMPLOYMENT DATA FROM THE 1960 DECENNIAL CENSUS OF POPULATION AND WAGE AND SALARY DATA FROM THE U.S. OFFICE OF BUSINESS ECONOMICS

The estimates in Table B–5 rely on the same wage and salary information that was used in Table B–4 and in Table 7 in Chapter III. The employment data are taken from the Decennial Census of Population, as in Table 7. As described in Chapter III, these data have weaknesses that limit their usefulness in measuring relative wage levels: no allowance is made for varying skill levels or for a larger proportion of multiple-job holders, for example.

The use of Decennial Census employment statistics has the following additional disadvantages:

1. *Decennial Census employment data usually are not comparable with U.S. Office of Business Economics wage and salary data for individual employment sectors.* The employee classifies himself in the Decennial Census as to whether or not he is employed and the type of employment. On the other hand, wage and salary information is coded and classified by the U.S. Bureau of Employment Security and other governmental agencies which obtain payroll reports from employers. Because the two series (payrolls and employment) are not necessarily consistent for *each employment sector,* the resulting figures on earnings per employee in each sector are probably biased.

2. *The Decennial Census provides information as of one point in time, April 15, 1960.* These data are not representative of employ-

TABLE B-5

Average Earnings per Person Employed, in Various Employment Sectors:
New England, United States Unadjusted, and United States Weighted to Reflect
New England's Composition of Employment
1960

Employment Sector	NEW ENGLAND		UNITED STATES	
	Percentage of Total Employed	*Wage and Salary Amount per Person*	*Wage and Salary Amount per Person*	*Amount per Person at New England Weights*
Total Employed	100.0	$4,825	$4,780	$4,807
Military	2.5	4,618	4,660	116
Total Civilian Employed	97.5	4,831	4,784	4,691
Proprietors, total	8.6	6,094	6,095	561
Agricultural	0.9	5,284	4,677	43
Nonagricultural	7.7	6,191	6,774	519
Wage and salaried, total	88.4	4,737	4,656	4,130
Agricultural	1.0	2,593	2,126	21
Nonagricultural	87.4	4,762	4,721	4,108
Mining	0.1	7,077	6,141	6
Contract construction	3.3	6,437	5,971	200
Manufacturing	34.6	4,992	5,168	1,787
Trade	13.4	5,469	5,108	686
Finance, insurance, real estate	4.0	5,652	5,341	211

See footnotes at end of table.

TABLE B–5 *(continued)*

Employment Sector	NEW ENGLAND		UNITED STATES	
	Percentage of Total Employed	Wage and Salary Amount per Person	Wage and Salary Amount per Person	Amount per Person at New England Weights
Transportation	2.4	$5,863	$6,075	$145
Communications, pub. utilities	2.2	5,644	5,640	125
Services	12.5	3,792	3,387	422
Government	10.7	4,732	4,843	516
Other	4.3	327	247	11
Unpaid family workers	0.5	—	—	—
Agricultural	0.1	—	—	—
Nonagricultural	0.4	—	—	—

NOTE: Detail may not add to total due to rounding.

SOURCES: Robert E. Graham, Jr., and Edwin J. Coleman, "Consumer Incomes Up in All Regions in 1960," *Survey of Current Business*, XLI (August, 1961), 14–15.

U.S. Bureau of the Census, *U.S. Census of Population: 1960. Detailed Characteristics.* Connecticut, Maine, Massachusetts, New Hampshire, Rhode Island, and Vermont (separate publication for each state) (Series PC[1]) (Washington, D.C.: U.S. Government Printing Office, 1962), Tables 115 and 129.

———, *U.S. Census of Population: 1960. General Social and Economic Characteristics, United States Summary* (Series PC[1]) (Washington, D.C.: U.S. Government Printing Office, 1962), Tables 83 and 86.

———, *U.S. Census of Population: 1960.* Advance copy of Table 214, "Industry of the Employed, by Class of Worker and Sex, for the United States: 1960" (Washington, D.C.: The Bureau, 1962).

ment throughout the year, and only a partial adjustment can be made for this defect by dividing the April 15 employment data by the appropriate April monthly seasonal adjustment factor.

3. *Decennial Census employment data are based on the residence of each employee and not the location of his work.* Many persons who work in New York City reside in Fairfield County, Connecticut, and are included as Connecticut employees in the Decennial Census of Population. Similarly, the U.S. Office of Business Economics makes an adjustment in the Connecticut wage and salary figures for income earned in New York City. The resulting figures for earnings per employee are, therefore, representative of Connecticut *and* part of New York City. For the purposes of this book, only data for earnings of persons employed within the boundaries of Connecticut are relevant.

On the other hand, the information from the Decennial Census does have two strong points:

1. *It provides complete coverage for each state for unemployment and for all categories of employment.* All other state employment series exclude unemployment and at least one category of employment. For example, the U.S. Bureau of Labor Statistics state employment series excludes agricultural employment.

2. *There is no double counting of employment.* Each employee reports only his primary employment. In other series, an employed person is counted twice if he works for two employers who report to the same data-collection agency.

We have no good method for judging the over-all accuracy of relative wage-level figures for New England shown in Table B–5. However, the procedures used in collecting Decennial Census employment data suggest that other employment series are more reliable. Furthermore, these other sources of information generally provide consistent results, while Decennial Census employment data provide what appear to be very high relative earnings estimates. It is the author's judgment that these estimates of New England earnings are exaggerated by 2 or 3 percentage points.

APPENDIX C

WEIGHTING VALUE ADDED PER MAN-HOUR[1]

The Problem

Between 1947 and 1958 New England manufacturing had a relative decline in "productivity." Table 18 shows that by 1963, value added per man-hour in the region was only 83.5 per cent of that in the nation.

These data might be interpreted to mean that New England manufacturers use outmoded production techniques and equipment or that the region's labor force is inefficient. No conclusions can be drawn, however, unless the national data are adjusted for New England's manufacturing specialization. This Appendix provides an explanation of the method used in this book to calculate "what value added per man-hour in all manufacturing in the United States would be if the nation produced the type of products manufactured in New England."[2]

Collecting Comparable Data

In this book the national productivity data are adjusted for New England specialization on a four-digit basis. A more detailed adjustment would have been desirable, but manufacturing statistics are not available on a five-digit basis.

Weighting the National Data

The weighting system used in this book simulates an economy

---

1. I am indebted to Mr. David F. Bradford for substantial assistance in developing the weighting system described in this Appendix. Mr. Bradford, a graduate student at Stanford University, worked in the Research Department of the Federal Reserve Bank of Boston in the summer of 1961.

2. See Chapter VI, pages 82 and 88.

with New England output and national productivity in each four-digit industry. The number of man-hours required to produce the value added in the ith four-digit industry in New England with national value added per man-hour in the same four-digit industry can be calculated as follows:

$y_{N.E._i}$ = value added by manufacture in the ith four-digit industry in New England.

$y_{U.S._i}$ = value added by manufacture in the ith four-digit industry in the United States.

$x_{U.S._i}$ = man-hours in the ith four-digit industry in the United States.

$\dfrac{y_{U.S._i}}{x_{U.S._i}} = p_{U.S._i}$ = United States productivity or value added per man-hour in the ith four-digit industry.

$\dfrac{y_{N.E._i}}{p_{U.S._i}} = x_{H_i}$ = man-hours required to produce the output of a hypothetical ith four-digit industry with New England value added and United States productivity.

The total number of man-hours required (X_H) in the hypothetical two-digit industry with n four-digit components is:

$$\sum_{i=1}^{n} \frac{y_{N.E._i}}{p_{U.S._i}} = \sum_{i=1}^{n} x_{H_i} = X_H$$

The average productivity (P) in this hypothetical two-digit industry can then be calculated:

$$\frac{\sum\limits_{i=1}^{n} y_{N.E._i}}{\sum\limits_{i=1}^{n} x_{H_i}} = \frac{\sum\limits_{i=1}^{n} y_{N.E._i}}{X_H} = P$$

This average productivity for the hypothetical two-digit industry is the same as that obtained by weighting United States productivity, $p_{U.S._i}$, for each four-digit component by the four-digit distribution of total hypothetical man-hours (X_H) and summing the products, since

$$P = \frac{\sum\limits_{i=1}^{n} y_{N.E._i}}{\sum\limits_{i=1}^{n} x_{H_i}} = \frac{\sum\limits_{i=1}^{n} y_{N.E._i}}{X_H} =$$

$$\sum_{i=1}^{n} y_{N\,E._i} \cdot \frac{1}{X_H} = \sum_{i=1}^{n} \left[\frac{y_{N.E._i}}{x_{H_i}} \cdot \frac{x_{H_i}}{X_H} \right]$$

where

$$\frac{y_{N.E._i}}{x_{H_i}} = p_{U.S._i}$$

and

$\dfrac{x_{H_i}}{X_H}$ = the percentage weight for hypothetical man-hours for each four-digit component of the hypothetical two-digit industry.

An easier way to compute P is to calculate its inverse $\dfrac{1}{P}$, which represents the average amount of time, or fraction of a man-hour, required to produce a dollar of value added in the same hypothetical two-digit industry consisting of n four-digit components with New England value added and national productivity. Thus, $\dfrac{1}{P}$ is a weighted average of the amounts of time required to produce a dollar of value added in each four-digit component. In this case, the appropriate percentage weights are those for the distribution of value added by four-digit components in New England. These weights (w_i) are calculated:

$$w_i = \frac{y_{N.E._i}}{\sum\limits_{i=1}^{n} y_{N.E._i}} = \frac{y_{N.E._i}}{Y_{N.E.}}$$

where $Y_{N.E.}$ is the total value added in the two-digit industry in New England.

When each weight is multiplied by the inverse of the national productivity $\left(\dfrac{1}{p_{U.S._i}}\right)$ for the same four-digit component, and the products are summed, the result is:

$$\sum_{i=1}^{n} w_i \cdot \frac{1}{p_{U.S._i}} = \frac{1}{P}$$

As before, in the calculation of P

$$\frac{1}{P} = \frac{\displaystyle\sum_{i=1}^{n} x_{H_i}}{\displaystyle\sum_{i=1}^{n} y_{N.E._i}} = \frac{\displaystyle\sum_{i=1}^{n} x_{H_i}}{Y_{N.E.}} =$$

$$\sum_{i=1}^{n} x_{H_i} \cdot \frac{1}{Y_{N.E.}} = \sum_{i=1}^{n} \left[\frac{x_{H_i}}{y_{N.E._i}} \cdot \frac{y_{N.E._i}}{Y_{N.E.}} \right]$$

where

$$\frac{y_{N.E._i}}{Y_{N.E.}} = w_i$$

and

$$\frac{x_{H_i}}{y_{N.E._i}} = \frac{1}{p_{U.S._i}}$$

BIBLIOGRAPHY

Government Publications

Board of Governors of the Federal Reserve System. *Industrial Production: 1959 Revision.* Washington, D.C.: The Board, 1960.

Committee on the New England Economy of the U.S. Council of Economic Advisers. *The New England Economy: A Report to the President . . .* Washington, D.C.: U.S. Government Printing Office, 1951.

U.S. Army. Corps of Engineers. *Waterborne Commerce of the United States: Calendar Year 1960.* Part I. *Waterways and Harbors—Atlantic Coast.* New York: U.S. Army. Corps of Engineers, North Atlantic Division, [1962].

————. *Waterborne Commerce of the United States: Calendar Year 1963.* Part I. *Waterways and Harbors—Atlantic Coast.* New York: U.S. Army. Corps of Engineers, North Atlantic Division, [1964].

U.S. Bureau of the Census. *Annual Survey of Manufactures: 1960.* Series M60 (AS). Washington, D.C.: U.S. Government Printing Office, 1962.

————. *Annual Survey of Manufactures: 1962.* Washington, D.C.: U.S. Government Printing Office, 1964.

————. *County and City Data Book, 1962: A Statistical Abstract Supplement.* Washington, D.C.: U.S. Government Printing Office, 1962.

————. "Components of Population Change, 1950 to 1960, for Counties, Standard Metropolitan Statistical Areas, State Economic Areas, and Economic Subregions." *Current Population Reports,* Series P-23, No. 7. Washington, D.C.: U.S. Government Printing Office, 1962.

————. "Preliminary Estimates of the Components of Population Change, by States: 1950 to 1960." *Current Population Reports,* Series P-25, No. 227. Washington, D.C.: U.S. Government Printing Office, 1961.

————. "Governmental Finances in 1960." *Governmental Finances in the United States.* Washington, D.C.: U.S. Government Printing Office, 1961.

————. "Governmental Finances in 1963." *Governmental Finances in the United States.* Washington, D.C.: U.S. Government Printing Office, 1964.

————. *Statistical Abstract of the United States: 1962.* (83d. ed.) Washingon, D.C.: U.S. Government Printing Office, 1962.

————. *Statistical Abstract of the United States: 1964.* (85th ed.) Washington, D.C.: U.S. Government Printing Office, 1964.

————. *U.S. Census of Agriculture: 1959*. Washington, D.C.: U.S. Government Printing Office, 1962.

————. *U.S. Census of Business: 1948*. Washington, D.C.: U.S. Government Printing Office, 1952.

————. *U.S. Census of Business: 1958*. Washington, D.C.: U.S. Government Printing Office, 1961.

————. *Census of Business: 1963*. Washington, D.C.: U.S. Government Printing Office, 1965.

————. *Census of Manufactures: 1947*. Washington, D.C.: U.S. Government Printing Office, 1949-1950.

————. *U.S. Census of Manufactures: 1954*. Washington, D.C.: U.S. Government Printing Office, 1957.

————. *U.S. Census of Manufactures: 1958*. Washington, D.C.: U.S. Government Printing Office, 1961.

————. *Census of Manufactures: 1963*. Washington, D.C.: U.S. Government Printing Office, 1964-1966.

————. *U.S. Census of Mineral Industries: 1958*. Washington, D.C.: U.S. Government Printing Office, 1961.

————. *Fourteenth Census of the United States: 1920*. Vol. III, *Population*. Washington, D.C.: U.S. Government Printing Office, 1922.

————. *U.S. Census of Population: 1950*. Washington, D.C.: U.S. Government Printing Office, 1951-1954.

————. *U.S. Census of Population: 1960*. Washington, D.C.: U.S. Government Printing Office, 1961.

U.S. Bureau of Employment Security. *Area Labor Market Trends, 1959-1960*.

————. *The Labor Market and Employment Security, 1948-1960*.

U.S. Bureau of Labor Statistics. *Consumer Price Index, October 1965: U.S. City Average and Selected Areas*. Washington, D.C.: The Bureau [November 30, 1965 release].

————. *Consumer Price Index—U.S.: All Items, 1913 Forward—Series A (1957-59 = 100)*. Washington, D.C.: The Bureau [1962 release].

————. *Employment and Earnings, Annual Supplement Issue*, VIII, No. 6 (November, 1961) and VIII, No. 12 (June, 1962).

————. *Employment and Earnings Statistics for States and Areas: 1939-64*. (Bulletin No. 1370-2.) Washington, D.C.: U.S. Government Printing Office, 1965.

————. *Employment and Earnings Statistics for the United States: 1909-1960*. (Bulletin No. 1312.) Washington, D.C.: U.S. Government Printing Office, 1961.

————. *Industry Wage Survey: Machinery Manufacturing, March-May 1961*. (Bulletin No. 1309.) Washington, D.C.: U.S. Government Printing Office, 1961.

————. *Industry Wage Survey: Machinery Manufacturing, March-May 1964*. (Bulletin No. 1429.) Washington, D.C.: U.S. Government Printing Office, 1965.

————. *Monthly Report on the Labor Force* (December, 1965).

————. *Prices: A Chartbook 1953-62.* (Bulletin No. 1351.) Washington, D.C.: U.S. Government Printing Office, December, 1962.

————. *Retail Prices and Indexes of Fuels and Electricity: October 1962.* Washington, D.C.: The Bureau [1962 release].

————. *State Employment: 1939-1956.* Washington, D.C.: U.S. Government Printing Office [1958].

————. *Wages and Related Benefits: 82 Labor Markets, 1960-1961.* (Bulletin No. 1285-83.) Washington, D.C.: U.S. Government Printing Office, 1961.

————. *Wages and Related Benefits: 40 Labor Markets, 1951-1952.* (Bulletin No. 1113.) Washington, D.C.: U.S. Government Printing Office [1952].

————. *Wages and Related Benefits in the Machinery Industries: Postwar Wage Trends. Survey of 20 Labor Markets, 1953-54.* (Bulletin No. 1160.) Washington, D.C.: U.S. Government Printing Office [1954].

————. *Wages and Related Benefits: Metropolitan Areas, United States and Regional Summaries, 1960-61.* (Bulletin No. 1285-84.) Washington, D.C.: U.S. Government Printing Office, 1962.

————. *Wages and Related Benefits.* Part I: *80 Metropolitan Areas, 1963-64.* Part II: *Metropolitan Areas, United States and Regional Summaries, 1963-64.* (Bulletin No. 1385-82.) Washington, D.C.: U.S. Government Printing Office, 1964-65.

————. *Wage Structure: Electric and Gas Utilities, September 1957.* (Report No. 135.) Washington, D.C.: U.S. Government Printing Office, 1958.

————. *Wage Structure: Pulp, Paper and Paperboard, April 1952.* (Series 2, No. 91.) Washington, D.C.: U.S. Government Printing Office, 1952.

U.S. Bureau of Labor Statistics, New England Regional Office. *Employment in New England: 1947-1961.* Boston: The Bureau, 1962.

U.S. Bureau of Mines. *Minerals Yearbook 1963.* Vol. III, *Area Reports: Domestic.* Washington, D.C.: U.S. Government Printing Office, 1964.

U.S. Department of Agriculture, Farm Economics Division. *Major Uses of Land and Water.* (Agricultural Economics Report No. 13.) Washington, D.C.: U.S. Government Printing Office, 1962.

U.S. Fish and Wildlife Service. *Fishery Statistics of the United States: 1950. Statistical Digest 27,* by A. W. Anderson and C. E. Peterson. Washington, D.C.: U.S. Government Printing Office, 1953.

————. *Fishery Statistics of the United States: 1960. Statistical Digest 53,* by E. A. Power. Washington, D.C.: U.S. Government Printing Office, 1962.

————. *Fishery Statistics of the United States: 1963.* Washington, D.C.: U.S. Government Printing Office, 1965.

U.S. Forest Service. *Timber Resources for America's Future.* (Forest

Resource Report No. 14.) Washington, D.C.: U.S. Government Printing Office, January, 1958.

————. *Timber Trends in the United States.* (Forest Resource Report No. 17.) Washington, D.C.: U.S. Government Printing Office, February, 1965.

U.S. Office of Business Economics. *National Income: A Supplement to the Survey of Current Business.* (1954 ed.) Washington, D.C.: U.S. Government Printing Office, 1954.

————. *Personal Income by States since 1929: A Supplement to the Survey of Current Business.* Washington, D.C.: U.S. Government Printing Office, 1956.

Books

Black, John Donald. *The Rural Economy of New England.* Cambridge, Mass.: Harvard University Press, 1950.

Clark, Colin. *The Conditions of Economic Progress.* London: Macmillan, 1940.

Committee of New England of the National Planning Association. *The Economic State of New England.* New Haven: Yale University Press, 1954.

Cunningham, William Glenn. *The Aircraft Industry: A Study in Industrial Location.* Los Angeles: L. L. Morrison, 1951.

Duesenberry, James S. *Business Cycles and Economic Growth.* New York: McGraw-Hill Book Co., Inc., 1958.

Dunlop, John T. "Productivity and the Wage Structure," in Metzler, L. A. et al., *Income, Employment, and Public Policy: Essays in Honor of Alvin H. Hansen.* New York: W. W. Norton, 1948, pp. 341-362.

————. *Wage Determination Under Trade Unions.* New York: The Macmillan Company, 1944.

Estall, R. C. *New England, A Study in Industrial Adjustment.* London: G. Bell and Sons, Ltd., 1966.

Friedman, M. "Some Comments on the Significance of Labor Unions for Economic Policy," Institute on the Structure of the Labor Market, American University, Washington, D.C., 1950. In John Maurice Clark et al., *The Impact of the Union: Eight Economic Theorists Evaluate the Labor Union Movement.* David McCord Wright, ed. New York: Harcourt, Brace and Co., 1951, pp. 204-234.

Fuchs, Victor R. *Changes in the Location of Manufacturing in the United States Since 1929.* New Haven: Yale University Press, 1962.

Goodrich, Carter, et al. *Migration and Economic Opportunity: The Report of the Study of Population Redistribution.* Philadelphia: University of Pennsylvania Press, 1936.

Gottman, Jean. *Megalopolis: The Urbanized Northeastern Seaboard of the United States.* New York: The Twentieth Century Fund, 1961.

Greenhut, Melvin L. *Plant Location in Theory and in Practise: The Eco-*

nomics of Space. Chapel Hill, N.C.: The University of North Carolina Press, 1956.

Handlin, Oscar. *Boston's Immigrants, 1790-1865; A Study in Acculturation*. Cambridge, Mass.: Harvard University Press, 1941.

Hanna, Frank A. *State Income Differentials: 1919-1954*. Durham, N. C.: Duke University Press, 1959.

Harris, Seymour E. *The Economics of New England*. Cambridge, Mass.: Harvard University Press, 1952.

Hartland, Penelope C. *Balance of Interregional Payments of New England*. (Brown University Studies, Vol. XIV.) Providence: Brown University, 1950.

Hoover, Edgar M. *Location Theory and the Shoe and Leather Industries*. Cambridge, Mass.: Harvard University Press, 1937.

Hutchinson, Edward P. *Immigrants and Their Children, 1850-1950*. New York: John Wiley & Sons, Inc., 1956.

International Economic Association. *The Theory of Wage Determination*. (Proceedings of a conference held by the International Economic Association. Edited by John T. Dunlop.) New York: St. Martin's Press, 1957.

Kennedy, Thomas. *The Significance of Wage Uniformity*. Philadelphia: University of Pennsylvania Press, 1949.

Kuznets, Simon; Miller, Ann Ratner; and Easterlin, Richard A. *Population Redistribution and Economic Growth: United States, 1870-1950*. Vol. II. *Analyses of Economic Change*. Philadelphia: The American Philosophical Society, 1960.

Lee, Everett S. *et al. Population Redistribution and Economic Growth: United States, 1870-1950*. Vol. I. *Methodological Considerations and Reference Tables*. Philadelphia: The American Philosophical Society, 1957.

Lester, Richard A. *Labor and Industrial Relations*. New York: The Macmillan Company, 1951.

Lester, Richard A., and Shister, Joseph (eds.). *Insights into Labor Issues*. New York: The Macmillan Company, 1949.

Long, Clarence D. *The Labor Force under Changing Income and Employment*. (A Study by the National Bureau of Economic Research, Number 65, General Series.) Princeton, N. J.: Princeton University Press, 1958.

Mayer, Kurt B. *Economic Development and Population Growth in Rhode Island*. (Brown University Papers, Vol. XXVIII.) Providence: Brown University, 1953.

Miernyk, William H. *Inter-Industry Labor Mobility: The Case of the Displaced Textile Worker*. Boston: Northeastern University, Bureau of Business and Economic Research, 1955.

Palmer, Gladys L. *Labor Mobility in Six Cities; A Report on the Survey* of Patterns and Factors in Labor Mobility, 1940-1950. New York: Social Science Research Council, 1954.

Parnes, Herbert S. *Research on Labor Mobility: An Appraisal of Research Findings in the United States*. (Bulletin 65.) New York: Social Science Research Council, 1954.

Perloff, Harvey S. *et al. Regions, Resources, and Economic Growth*. Baltimore: Johns Hopkins Press, 1960.

Pittsburgh Regional Planning Association. *Region in Transition*. Pittsburgh, Penna.: University of Pittsburgh Press, 1963.

Reder, M. W. "Wage Determination in Theory and Practice," in *A Decade of Industrial Relations Research*. Chamberlain, Neil W.; Pierson, Frank C.; and Wolfson, Theresa, eds. New York: Harper [1958], pp. 64-98.

Reynolds, Lloyd G. *Labor Economics and Labor Relations*. 2d ed. revised. Englewood Cliffs, N. J.: Prentice-Hall, Inc., 1956.

————. *The Structure of Labor Markets*. New York: Harper and Brothers, 1951.

Reynolds, Lloyd G., and Taft, Cynthia H. *The Evolution of Wage Structure*. New Haven: Yale University Press, 1956.

Robinson, Joan. *Essays in the Theory of Employment*. 2d. ed. revised. Oxford: Basil Blackwell, 1947.

Rothschild, K. W. *The Theory of Wages*. New York: The Macmillan Company, 1954.

Segal, Martin. *Wages in the Metropolis: Their Influence on the Location of Industries in the New York Region*. Cambridge, Mass.: Harvard University Press, 1960.

Shepard, H. B. *Hardwood Pulp: Its Manufacture and Use*. Boston: The New England Council, 1956.

Shipman, William D. *An Inquiry into the High Cost of Electricity in New England*. Middletown, Conn.: Wesleyan University Press, 1962.

Taylor, George W., and Pierson, Frank C. (eds.). *New Concepts in Wage Determination*. New York: McGraw-Hill Book Co., Inc., 1957.

Truesdell, Leon E. *The Canadian Born in the United States: An Analysis of the Statistics of the Canadian Element in the Population of the United States, 1850 to 1930*. New Haven: Yale University Press, 1943.

Vernon, Raymond. *Metropolis, 1985: An Interpretation of the Findings of the New York Metropolitan Region Study*. Cambridge, Mass.: Harvard University Press, 1960.

White, Donald J. *The New England Fishing Industry: A Study in Price and Wage Setting*. Cambridge, Mass.: Harvard University Press, 1954.

Wright, John K. *New England's Prospect: 1933*. (American Geographical Society Special Publication No. 16.) New York: American Geographical Society, 1933.

Articles and Periodicals

"Achieving Success in Specialty Paper," *New England Business Review: Federal Reserve Bank of Boston,* September, 1960, pp. 1-4.

Anderson, Paul S. "The Apparent Decline in Capital-Output Ratios," *The Quarterly Journal of Economics,* LXXV (November, 1961), 615-634.

Bell, Frederick W. "A Note on the Empirical Estimation of the CES Production Function with the Use of Capital Data," *The Review of Economics and Statistics,* XLVII (August, 1965), 328-330.

————. "Changing Specialization and Bay State Growth," *New England Business Review: Federal Reserve Bank of Boston,* April, 1965, pp. 2-8.

Bloch, Joseph W. "Regional Wage Differentials: 1907-46," *Monthly Labor Review,* LXVI (April, 1948), 371-377.

[Bright, Jr., Arthur A.]. "Industrial Power Costs in New England," *Monthly Review: Federal Reserve Bank of Boston,* XXXII (June, 1950), 1-13.

Coleman, Edwin J. "Personal Income by States in 1961," *Survey of Current Business,* XLII (August, 1962), 8-17.

Cullen, Donald E. "The Interindustry Wage Structure, 1899-1950," *The American Economic Review,* XLVI (June, 1956), 353-369.

Davis, Lance Edwin. "Stock Ownership in the Early New England Textile Industry," *The Business History Review,* XXXII (Summer, 1958), 204-222.

Eckstein, Otto, and Wilson, Thomas A. "Determination of Money Wages in American Industry," *The Quarterly Journal of Economics,* LXXVI (August, 1962), 379-414.

E. H. Boeckh and Associates, Inc. "Cost Indexes for 10 Types of Buildings," *Engineering News-Record,* March 22, 1962, p. 85 and March 18, 1965, p. 90.

[Eisenmenger, Robert W.]. "Industrial Fuel Costs in New England," *New England Business Review: Federal Reserve Bank of Boston,* August, 1957, pp. 1-4, October, 1957, pp. 5-7.

"ENR Costs Report and Outlook," *Engineering News-Record,* Dec. 20, 1962, pp. 59-104.

Ernst, Harry. "Accounting for Productivity Changes," *Harvard Business Review,* XXXIV (May-June, 1956), 109-121.

Estle, Edwin F. "Electronics on the Move," *New England Business Review: Federal Reserve Bank of Boston,* January, 1966, pp. 11-15.

————. "New England's Wage Level Approaches National Average," *New England Business Review: Federal Reserve Bank of Boston,* March, 1966, pp. 2-7.

Ferguson, C. E. "Cross-Section Production Functions and the Elasticity of Substitution in American Manufacturing Industry," *The Review of Economics and Statistics,* XLV (August, 1963), 305-313.

Fischer, John. "The Editor's Easy Chair," *Harper's Magazine,* CCXXIII (September, 1961).

Fuchs, Victor R., and Perlman, Richard. "Recent Trends in Southern Wage Differentials," *The Review of Economics and Statistics,* XLII (August, 1960), 292-300.

Garbarino, Joseph W. "A Theory of Interindustry Wage Structure Variation," *The Quarterly Journal of Economics,* LXIV (May, 1950), 282-305.

[Gooding, Edwin C.]. "Area Redevelopment Act in New England," *New England Business Review: Federal Reserve Bank of Boston,* April, 1962, pp. 1-4.

Graham, Jr., Robert E., and Coleman, Edwin J. "Consumer Incomes Up in All Regions in 1960," *Survey of Current Business,* XLI (August, 1961), 9-19.

Haddy, Pamela, and Tolles, N. Arnold. "British and American Changes in Interindustry Wage Structure under Full Employment," *The Review of Economics and Statistics,* XXXIX (November, 1957), 408-414.

Hansen, W. L. "The Cyclical Sensitivity of the Labor Supply," *The American Economic Review,* LI (June, 1961), 299-309.

Hunter, Helen M. "Innovation, Competition, and Locational Changes in the Pulp and Paper Industry: 1880-1950," *Land Economics,* XXXI (November, 1955), 314-327.

"Investment and Productivity in New England Manufacturing Industries: Part I, The Background," *New England Business Review: Federal Reserve Bank of Boston,* January, 1960, pp. 7-9.

Kanninen, Toivo P. "Occupational Wage Relationships in Manufacturing, 1952-53," *Monthly Labor Review,* LXXVI (November, 1953), 1171-1178.

Katona, George, and Morgan, James N. "The Quantitative Study of Factors Determining Business Decisions," *The Quarterly Journal of Economics,* LXVI (February, 1952), 67-90.

Keesing, Donald B. "Labor Skills and International Trade: Evaluating Many Trade Flows with a Single Measuring Device," *The Review of Economics and Statistics,* LXVII (August, 1965), 287-294.

Kerr, Clark. "The Balkanization of Labor Markets," Bakke, E. Wight. *Labor Mobility and Economic Opportunity.* Cambridge, Mass.: Technology Press of Massachusetts Institute of Technology, 1954, pp. 92-110.

Lamale, Helen H., and Stotz, Margaret S. "The Interim City Worker's Family Budget," *Monthly Labor Review,* LXXXIII (August, 1960), 785-808.

Lebergott, Stanley. "Long Term Factors in Labor Mobility and Unemployment," *Monthly Labor Review,* LXXXII (August, 1959), 876-881.

————. "Wage Structures," *The Review of Economics and Statistics,* XXIX (November, 1947), 274-285.

Leontief, Wassily. "Domestic Production and Foreign Trade; The American Capital Position Re-examined," in Proceedings of the American Philosophical Society, September 28, 1953. Reprinted in *Economia Internazionale,* Genoa (1954), No. 1.

Lester, Richard A. "Effectiveness of Factory Labor: South-North Comparisons," *Journal of Political Economy,* LIV (February, 1946), 60-75.

————. "A Range Theory of Wage Differentials," *Industrial and Labor Relations Review,* V (July, 1952), 483-500.

————. "Wage Diversity and Its Theoretical Implications," *The Review of Economic Statistics,* XXVIII (August, 1946), 152-159.

Maher, J. D. "Union, Non-Union Wage Differentials," *The American Economic Review,* XLVI (June, 1956), 336-352.

Maher, John E. "Wages: The Pattern of Wage Movement in the United States Since 1945—Its Meaning and Significance," *The Review of Economics and Statistics,* XLIII (August, 1961), 277-282.

McCaffree, Kenneth M. "The Earnings Differential between White Collar and Manual Occupations," *The Review of Economics and Statistics,* XXXV (February, 1953), 20-30.

Marcus, Matityahu. "Capital-Labor Substitution Among States: Some Empirical Evidence," *The Review of Economics and Statistics,* XLVI (November, 1964), 434-438.

Neal, Alfred C. "From the Bookshelf: Problems Still to be Solved," (A review of Seymour E. Harris, *The Economics of New England*) *The Christian Science Monitor,* May 13, 1952.

"New England Manufacturing . . . Its Future Prospects," *Monthly Review: Federal Reserve Bank of Boston,* XXXI (September, 1949), 1-11.

Ober, Harry. "Occupational Wage Differentials, 1907-1947," *Monthly Labor Review,* LXVII (August, 1948), 127-134.

Ostry, Sylvia W. "Interindustry Earnings Differentials in Canada, 1945-1956," *Industrial and Labor Relations Review,* XII (April, 1959), 335-352.

Raimon, Robert L. "Interstate Migration and Wage Theory," *The Review of Economics and Statistics,* XLIV (November, 1962), 428-438.

Reder, M. W. "The Theory of Occupational Wage Differentials," *The American Economic Review,* XLV (December, 1955), 833-852.

[Rieber, Michael]. "Crude Oil Imports Restrictions," *New England Business Review: Federal Reserve Bank of Boston,* November, 1961, pp. 1-4.

Ross, Arthur M., and Goldner, William. "Forces Affecting the Interindustry Wage Structure," *The Quarterly Journal of Economics,* LXIV (May, 1950), 254-281.

"The Roving Population," *New England Business Review: Federal Reserve Bank of Boston,* October, 1960, pp. 6-7.

Samuelson, Paul A. "International Trade and the Equalization of Factor Prices," *Economic Journal,* LVIII (June, 1948), 163-184.

Segal, Martin. "Interrelationship of Wages Under Joint Demand: The Case of the Fall River Textile Workers," *The Quarterly Journal of Economics,* LXX (August, 1956), 464-477.

————. "Regional Wage Differences in Manufacturing in the Postwar Period," *The Review of Economics and Statistics,* XLIII (May, 1961), 148-155.

[Shen, T. Y.]. "Investment and Productivity in New England Manufacturing Industries: Part 1, The Background," *New England Business Review: Federal Reserve Bank of Boston,* January, 1960, pp. 7-9.

Shultz, George P. "Recent Research on Labor Mobility," Industrial Relations Research Association. *Proceedings of the Fourth Annual Meeting. Boston, Mass., Dec. 28-29, 1951.* Edited by L. Reed Tripp. Madison, Wisconsin: The Association, 1952, pp. 110-118.

Slichter, Sumner H. "Notes on the Structure of Wages," *The Review of Economics and Statistics,* XXXII (February, 1950), 80-91.

Sobel, Irvin, and Wilcock, Richard C. "Labor Market Behavior in Small Towns," *Industrial and Labor Relations Review,* IX (October, 1955), 54-76.

Sobotka, Stephen P. "Michigan's Employment Problem: The Substitution Against Labor," *The Journal of Business,* XXXIV (April, 1961), 119-128.

Stotz, Margaret S. "The BLS Interim Budget for a Retired Couple," *Monthly Labor Review,* LXXXIII (November, 1960), 1141-1157.

"Textile Trends," *New England Business Review: Federal Reserve Bank of Boston,* December, 1960, pp. 5-7.

Ulman, L. "Marshall and Friedman on Union Strength," *The Review of Economics and Statistics,* XXXVII (November, 1955), 384-406.

[Walker, Richard A.]. "Is There A 'Prevailing Wage'?" *New England Business Review: Federal Reserve Bank of Boston,* December, 1961, pp. 1-4.

Wilkinson, John M. "New England Power Developments: Part 1 . . . the private utility industry," *New England Business Review: Federal Reserve Bank of Boston,* February, 1966, pp. 2-17.

Reports

Arthur D. Little, Inc. *Diversification: An Opportunity for the New England Textile Industry.* Boston: Federal Reserve Bank of Boston, 1955.

————. *Report on A Survey of Industrial Opportunities in New England to the Federal Reserve Bank of Boston.* Cambridge, Mass.: Arthur D. Little, Inc., 1952.

Ashton, David J. *New England Manufacturers' Export Practice and Potential.* (Research Report to the Federal Reserve Bank of Boston, No. 9.) Boston: Federal Reserve Bank of Boston, 1960.

Bell, Frederick W. *The Economics of the New England Fishing Industry: The Role of Technological Change and Government Aid.* (Research Report to the Federal Reserve Bank of Boston, No. 31.) Boston: Federal Reserve Bank of Boston, 1966.

Chamber of Commerce of the United States. *Fringe Benefits 1961.* (Research Study prepared by the Economic Research Department.) Washington, D.C.: The Chamber, 1962.

———. *Fringe Benefits 1963.* (Research Study prepared by the Economic Research Department.) Washington, D.C.: The Chamber, 1964.

Coughlin, Marguerite I. *Outlook for New England's Shoe Industry to 1970.* (Research Report to the Federal Reserve Bank of Boston: 1970 Projection No. 14.) Boston: Federal Reserve Bank of Boston, 1959.

Doody, Francis S. *The Immediate Economic Impact of Higher Education in New England.* (Education Studies, New Series, No. 1.) Boston: Boston University, Bureau of Business Research, 1961.

Edison Electric Institute. *Electric Utility Industry Statistics in the United States for the Year 1959.* New York: Edison Electric Institute, 1960.

———. *Statistical Year Book of the Electric Utility Industry for 1961.* New York: Edison Electric Institute, 1962.

———. *Statistical Year Book of the Electric Utility Industry for 1963.* New York: Edison Electric Institute, 1964.

Eisenmenger, Robert W. *Fuel and Energy Use in the 1960's.* (Research Report to the Federal Reserve Bank of Boston: 1970 Projection No. 9.) Boston: Federal Reserve Bank of Boston, 1959.

Federal Reserve Bank of Boston. *Annual Report, 1961: New England at Work in the Space Age.* Boston: Federal Reserve Bank of Boston, 1962.

Hendrick, Paul; Pfister, Richard L.; and Segal, Martin. *Vacation Travel Business in New Hampshire: A Survey and Analysis.* Concord, N. H.: New Hampshire Department of Resources and Economic Development, 1962.

Hodgson, Raphael W. *Interview Reports on the Effects of Trade Liberalization on New England Manufacturing.* (Research Report to the Federal Reserve Bank of Boston, No. 22.) Boston: Federal Reserve Bank of Boston, 1963.

Lindahl, Martin L. *Railroad Freight Rates and New England's Competitive Position.* (A Research Report to accompany Report No. 9 of the New England Governors' Committee on Public Transportation, *Public Transportation for New England.*) Boston: The Committee, 1957.

Miernyk, William H. *New England Textile Employment in 1970.* (Research Report to the Federal Reserve Bank of Boston: 1970 Projection No. 16.) Boston: Federal Reserve Bank of Boston, 1959.

Miernyk, William H., and Bright, Jr., Arthur A. *The Textile Industries of New England.* (Staff Memorandum No. 10 of the Committee of New England of the National Planning Association.) Boston: Federal Reserve Bank of Boston, 1952.

National Bureau of Economic Research. *Regional Income. Studies in Income and Wealth,* Volume Twenty-One, by the Conference on Research in Income and Wealth. Princeton, N. J.: Princeton University Press, 1957.

————. *Studies in Income and Wealth,* Volume Eleven, by the Conference on Research in Income and Wealth. New York: The Bureau, 1949.

New England Governors' Committee on Public Transportation. *Public Transportation for New England.* (A series of 10 reports to the New England Governors' Conference.) Boston: The Committee, 1957.

New England-New York Inter-Agency Committee. *The Resources of the New England-New York Region.* (Part I. *The General Report;* Part II. *The Technical Report,* in 39 chapters; Part III. *Reference Data,* in 3 volumes.) New York: The Committee, 1955.

Raphaelson, Arnold H.; Siedlik, Tadeusz A.; and Coupe, John D. *A Study of the Vacation Industry in Maine.* Orono, Maine: University of Maine, School of Business Administration, 1961.

Rieber, Michael. *Residual Oil Import Restrictions.* (Research Report to the Federal Reserve Bank of Boston, No. 16.) Boston: Federal Reserve Bank of Boston, 1961.

Robinson, Romney. "Water Transportation and New England: An Economic Survey of the New England Seaports." (A report to the New England Governors' Committee on Public Transportation.) *Public Transportation for New England. Report No. 8.* Boston: The Committee, 1957.

Rubenstein, Albert H., and Andrews, Victor L. *The Electronics Industry in New England to 1970.* (Research Report to the Federal Reserve Bank of Boston: 1970 Projection No. 4.) Boston: Federal Reserve Bank of Boston, 1959.

Ruggles, Richard. "The Nature of Price Flexibility and the Determinants of Relative Price Changes in the Economy," National Bureau of Economic Research, *Business Concentration and Price Policy.* A Conference of the Universities—National Bureau Committee for Economic Research. Princeton, N. J.: Princeton University Press, 1955.

Strasma, John D. *State and Local Taxation of Industry: Some Comparisons.* (Research Report to the Federal Reserve Bank of Boston, No. 4.) Boston: Federal Reserve Bank of Boston, 1959.

Walker, Richard A. *Wage Structure Patterns in a Metropolitan Area.* (Research Report to the Federal Reserve Bank of Boston, No. 18.) Boston: Federal Reserve Bank of Boston, 1961.

Unpublished Material

Barraclough, Solon L. "Forest Land Ownership in New England." Unpublished Ph.D. dissertation, Department of Economics, Harvard University, 1949.

Buehner, Ronald C. "The Effect of Walsh-Healey Minimum Wages on Regional Industries." Unpublished Master's thesis, School of Industrial Management, Massachusetts Institute of Technology, 1962.

Eisenmenger, Robert W. "Holyoke Water Power Company vs. Municipal Gas and Electric Department." Unpublished honors thesis, Department of Economics, Amherst College, 1949.

Ellis, George H. "Postwar Industrial Location in New England." Unpublished Ph.D. dissertation, Department of Economics, Harvard University, 1949.

Green, Howard L. "The Reach of New York City and Boston into Southern New England." Unpublished Ph.D. dissertation, Division of Geological Sciences, Harvard University, 1952.

Hughes, William H. "The Efficient Organization of the Privately Owned Electric Utility Industry in the United States." Unpublished Ph.D. dissertation, Department of Economics, Harvard University, 1959.

Hunter, Helen M. "United States International Trade in Wood Pulp: A Case Study in International Trade." Unpublished Ph.D. dissertation, Department of Economics, Harvard University, 1952.

McGouldrick, Paul Foster. "Profits, Capital, and Capital Spending in the New England Cotton Textile Industry of the 19th Century." Unpublished Ph.D. dissertation, Department of Economics, Harvard University, 1965.

Miernyk, William H. "Labor Cost and Labor Supply as Determinants of Industrial Location." Unpublished Ph.D. dissertation, Department of Economics, Harvard University, 1953.

Pardee, Scott E. "A Study of Intercity Wage Differentials." Unpublished Ph.D. dissertation, Department of Economics and Social Science, Massachusetts Institute of Technology, 1962.

Rich, Stuart U. "Product Policies of Nonintegrated New England Paper Companies." Unpublished Doctor of Business Administration dissertation, Graduate School of Business Administration, Harvard University, 1960.

Sjaastad, Larry A. "Income and Migration in the United States." Unpublished Ph.D. dissertation, Department of Economics, University of Chicago, 1961.

U.S. Bureau of Labor Statistics, New England Regional Office. Unpublished data for the New England states.

Wickman, Kenneth Paul. "Historical and Locational Aspects of Economic

Decline in the New England Furniture Industry." Unpublished Ph.D. dissertation, Department of Economics, Syracuse University, 1962.

Other Sources

Northern Textile Association. Personal Interview with Daniel Gordon, Boston, Mass. March 14, 1963.

U.S. Bureau of Labor Statistics, New England Regional Office. Personal interview with Joseph Conaty, Regional Price Economist, Boston, Mass. December 15, 1962.

INDEX

A Roman numeral/Arabic numeral refers to a note to be found in "Notes," pages 115–123 (e.g., I/1 refers to Chapter I, note 1). An Arabic numeral followed by "n" refers to a footnote to be found on the page given.

191